Champagne
& HashBrowns

Sharon Somerville Boyes

ISBN: 979-8-9940357-0-2 (Paperback)

ISBN: 979-8-9940357-1-9 (Hardcover)

ISBN: 979-8-9940357-2-6 (e-book)

ISBN: 979-8-9940357-3-3 (audio)

Printed in the United States of America

First edition printing, 2026

All inquiries about this book can be sent to the author at info@boyesofsomer.com

For more information or to book an event, visit the website www.boyesofsomer.com

This book is dedicated to:

Meggie, Marc, and my Boyes.

The many Guardian Angels watching over me,
the West Park Coven, and my beloved Echo Victor.

Cheers

"This above all:
to thine own self be true."
—William Shakespeare

Author's Note

I'VE BEEN WRITING this book for a very long time. Some of the things that have gotten in my way: not enough time, not enough self-worth, not enough clarity.

Life also kept handing me curve ball after curve ball. I seemed to go from crisis to crisis, with periods of "calm" in between—except those moments of calm were fraught with anxiety about what lurked next around the corner. Anxiety became my baseline quite early on. Always on high alert, this endless cycle affected my health, wealth, and self. These are the three key pillars I cling to when trying to "improve" or "fix" my life. Still do.

But when I would start writing things down, my busy brain made it difficult to concentrate or even focus enough to see where I wanted the story to go—or, heck, what was it really all about? Even this, my debut book, is a bit hard to define. It's part memoir, part manifesto. It's the story of an ordinary girl with an extraordinary number of interests. It's about being too loud while suffering in silence. It's about being too much, yet not enough. It's about things that seem like total opposites that surprisingly do, can, and should go together—like champagne and hashbrowns.

What this book isn't is a roadmap, a how-to, with worksheets, or a checklist of things that you need to do over the next 30–60–90 days to get it right or rewire your brain. It's meant to be thought-provoking, inspiring, and validating, while hopefully giving you a good laugh.

While we are not performing brain surgery here, this book does tackle some tough subjects that can have very real consequences—things that most of us don't like to talk about or have been taught we don't discuss in polite society, workplaces, or even within our own families. In other words: *We Don't Talk About Bruno.*

But these conversations are necessary. Especially as the world keeps moving faster and getting smaller, all while set to a soundtrack that's loud, imperfect, and impossible to ignore—one that begs the question Four Non Blondes once asked, *"What's Going On?"*

At least that's the question this blonde has been asking herself for decades. It wasn't until a personal reckoning—and more than a year in trauma therapy—that I finally had the clarity to see what I couldn't see before: the rusted signs I'd been ignoring all my life.

What follows isn't advice or instruction. It's story—told from a trauma-informed place, shaped by lived experience, and intentionally tinted with a rock & roll edge. If you're looking for neat and tidy, or all the answers, let me know when you find them.

My hope is that you'll see yourself somewhere in this mess and music and realize you are not alone.

That you matter.

And that it's okay not to be okay.

That you can rebuild and reinvent.

At any age.

To understand how I got here, you'll be introduced to the Somerville family. The Somervilles are deeply loving, wildly fun, and humanly flawed. It's a giant cast of characters, with the original thirteen sibling set spanning a twenty-year age gap from the youngest to the oldest. One early reader liked them so much she asked to be invited to the next family gathering.

These stories come to you as remembered, not reconstructed. Trauma distorts time, sequence, and certainty. The effects of that trauma are more important than providing a court transcript. I chose to honor that distortion rather than edit it away or go on a fact-finding mission to prove who's right.

One final note about alcohol. Alcohol has been a very destructive force in my life, and in so many others. While I personally love a good glass of Champagne, it serves as a powerful symbol. Champagne is usually reserved for special occasions. I'm calling bullshit on that. We only get one life. Life is meant to be lived with all the bubbles and sparkles. Every day is a gift and should be celebrated. Sprinkles are for winners.

So, grab a glass of whatever it is you drink, sit back, and enjoy the show. Cheers.

Contents

Content Note

THIS BOOK CONTAINS references to mental illness, childhood trauma, suicidal ideation, and institutionalization. These experiences are discussed from a personal and reflective perspective. Readers are encouraged to engage with this material in the way that feels safest for them.

Opening Act

I<small>T'S</small> D<small>ECEMBER</small> 23RD, and my Facebook post is the same as it has been for the past almost two decades I've been on this stupid platform. Some days I want to quit, but I manage social media for work, so I can't take a facebreak, or do a digital detox. And, like it or not, Facebook is still a valuable marketing channel.

It does have its upsides. Living in Florida, it's my link to my friends and family back in Ohio and across the nation. Plus, I was an early adopter, so I'm loyal, and the reality is, I'm comfortable here. I've resigned myself to the fact that this is what people my age use, as we scoff at the people who still use voicemail and sign their names to text messages. As our kids (and now grandkids...gulp) simultaneously scoff at us for being on Facebook while they've moved on to the newest, hippest social platform. And so it goes.

Happy xx birthday to my love, Eddie Vedder. Thank you so much for penning the most beautiful soundtrack to my life. Looking forward to seeing you and celebrating with you on the road soon. Keep on Rockin' in the Free World. 🩶

This post is usually accompanied by a photo from my most recent show. Or a personal favorite in my collection.

Music is a connector...a convener...a teacher...a friend.
Music is life.
And this is the story of mine.
I am mine.

Part 1:
Rusted Signs

Where It All Begins

Chapter 1:
The Day I Tried to Live

"I woke the same as any other day
Except a voice was in my head."
—Soundgarden, "The Day I Tried to Live"

"MY NAME IS Batman. And Robin is in my suitcase!" declared the little girl in 5C when the stewardess asked her name. She said it with such confidence; I almost believed her. This was a girl who knew who she was and feared nothing. Although she didn't look like Batman, she was just as fashionable. I mean you must admit, Batman has it all going on. The cape. The belt. The cowl. The car. But I digress.

Princess Batman looked like a living doll. She had green eyes, a raspberry pout, and gorgeous, long chestnut brown hair in loose curls. Tied up in a half-up pony with a thick strand of purple yarn. *Fun fact. Her hair is poker straight.* Her mom set her hair in sponge rollers every night. *No wonder I'm an insomniac.*

Her dress was a smart pantsuit. Purple Swiss-dot pleated smock top with a bow in the center of her tiny chest. Solid purple legging style pants flowed seamlessly into her black Mary Jane shoes with white-ruffled ankle socks. Careful thought and professional styling went into curating this version of Batman.

She was traveling as an unaccompanied minor, a much less foreign or frightening concept in the 1970s. Pre-9/11, air travel was much different. The most common security threat was

3

someone trying to smuggle something nefarious, like drugs, into the country. Or the person who "forgot" to take the gun out of their bag. Remember, the 9/11 hijackers were able to bring box cutters on the plane.

The 1970s were a time when you could bring your 5–14-year-old child to the airport, accompany him/her through security to their departure gate, and then wave goodbye at the window as the plane takes off with your child aboard. All the while comforted in the fact that minutes before, Princess Batman, was handed off to the nice Stewardess working First Class. Said stewardess would personally hand Princess Batman off to the family member waiting on the other end.

The unaccompanied minor program (is it a called a program?) still exist today. But you'll pay for the service. Age ranges and services vary per airline. Naturally, if you are flying lawn chair airlines (you know, the budget airlines), they only take unaccompanied minors 14+ because those minors, will really be on their own. Other more "upscale" airlines flying the friendly skies will provide slightly more service including at least a glass of water or even a pop. And they will escort the unaccompanied minor beyond the security check point to whomever is picking them up from the airport.

Sure, less scary in the 1970s, but let's unpack this for a minute. Shall we.

Who the f*ck puts an only child on a plane from Cleveland, Ohio, to Birmingham, Alabama, to spend the whole summer following yet another one of her mom's hospital stays in 4C a.k.a. the psyche ward? My family. That's who.

They meant well. It was a different time.

And, no worries, remember, "I'm Batman. And Robin is in my suitcase." I got this. *This isn't my first rodeo.*

For as long as I can remember, I've been putting on a brave front. Being a big girl about things that were wildly inappropriate for someone my age, armed only with the scraps of logic I pieced together from the limited guidance—or care—my mother could give. My father? A blank space on my birth certificate. In the words of Swift: *I got a blank space, baby... and I'll write your name.* And while I lived in a house full of people, I was very much facing this world alone. The world around me kept moving—loud, chaotic, indifferent—while I quietly learned how to survive in it. I read the room, read between the lines, read every sign that told me I was on my own.

I was considered a precocious child. I was curious as hell. Asked a lot of questions and made a lot of observations about the world around me.

Probably because I am always trying to stay one step ahead of what life is going to throw me next. I got very good - right quick, and even better with practice - at identifying the problem, coming up with a game plan, and telling myself several stories. Reinventing my own narrative. Putting on a mask.

I didn't know it then, but this was a system. A survival mechanism. One I built young and never fully dismantled.

As a result, I overplan and overthink everything. Because my goal is to avoid at all costs bringing out my backup plan. At age six, this plan solely rested on Robin (my teddy bear) in my suitcase. Robin was gifted to me two years earlier by my grandparents when I had to spend an overnight alone at Fairview Hospital to have my tonsils removed. Family-centered care wasn't a thing yet.

Robin was your classic brown Knickerbocker-style teddy bear with a cream-colored leather snout. He was the perfect touch, sensory object, and companion for my big night alone. Alone in a metal, high bar, pediatric crib on wheels that looked like something right off the old animal cracker boxes depicting circus animals in a cage.

Sure, I could tell him all my secrets and hash over all my plans with him. But he was my break glass in case of emergency. Breaking that glass would mean triggering the Bat signal that I MUST ask for help. A fate worse than death.

While "make-believe" is a something all children play, for me, my fantasies meant my survival and eventually my motivation. My consultations with Robin gave way to characters in books, art, fashion magazines, lyrics in music, and iconic movies, always in the pursuit of trying to figure out who I am. Trying to survive.

Never satisfied, I was constantly trying on different personas and chasing the next bright and shiny in the endless pursuit of the life I desire. A life where I fit in, belonged, wasn't watching from the side lines and didn't live in fear. A life where I didn't always need to be one step ahead. A life where I was safe and happy.

Robin was kept in my suitcase—not because I didn't need him, but because I couldn't afford for anyone to see that I needed comfort. Or, that I was scared shitless. Or, because I was a child, I didn't understand why I needed to be sent away. I couldn't understand why my mother couldn't care for me or why I didn't have a father. Or why people whispered the word "bastard" when speaking of me. Over and over again, I was being told I needed to be a big girl.

Smart as a whip, I understood the assignment. And would perform to perfection.

In my head, I firmly believed something must be wrong with me. I must be flawed. I mean why else wouldn't my father stick around? Why else couldn't I stay in Cleveland? Why else was my mom always in the hospital? Why? Why? Why? If I could just be brave, if I could be just better, if I could be just flawless, then I could be loved and safe.

So, I spent the next *five decades* giving every ounce of my thought and energy to studying the world around me in the endless pursuit of achieving perfection. Because once I was perfect, then there would be no more excuses. Nothing left to analyze. Nothing left to fix. And, if there is one thing I'm good at. It's being a student and a scholar. I love to learn. I love to perfect. I love nothing short of excellence. I wear it like metal I earned in combat. Because that is what life felt like, endless combat. *What else do you got for me?*

This type of lifestyle suited me until it didn't. Up until now, I took setbacks like a champ. I would course-correct and move on. This might mean suffering minor "situational depression," navigating a series of panic attacks, or even taking a step back in my career. I would be just fine! *No worries, Icarus, I got you. Problem-solving is my superpower.*

I would come out the other side, stronger, smarter, and sadly, often smaller.

Then one day. I was driving to work across the 9.9-mile Courtney Campbell Causeway connecting Clearwater to Tampa over the old Tampa Bay. I was in the throes of an incredibly deep depression and had been in it *for months* now. I was doing the work, but all the things I clung to at these times of trouble weren't working.

"Can't know what's high," Eddie Vedder sings in *Pendulum,* *"'til you've been down to so low."*

Driving, sobbing, Pearl Jam blaring from the stereo, watching the sun glistening on the waters, waiting, hoping to see a dolphin. To bring a smile to my face and be the sign of hope I so desperately needed from the universe. I had read somewhere that dolphins symbolize joy, protection, and resilience. It was a physical manifestation of my guardian angels.

It didn't come.

And there it was. The voice inside my head, *I just can't do this life anymore. I should just drive right off this damn bridge.*

This is not the first time suicidal ideation has crept into my brain. (I memorized *Resume* by Dorothy Parker in fifth grade). However, I've always managed to keep it at bay.

> *I mean, how selfish can you be?*
> *You have children.*
> *You are not your mother.*
> *She's the one who can't handle shit.*
> *You can.*

Then the whisper comes in like a siren's song.

> *But can you really? Can we really keep going like this?*

Anger takes the stage.

> *Look at you. You're a fucking mess!*
> *And the kids are alright.*

I drive for at least another mile, having that internal debate with myself. And, as a Shakespearean scholar, I am really, really good at dialogue, debate, and playing devil's advocate. *It's who I am. It's what I live for.* I can eviscerate someone with my sharp tongue in seconds flat, and there is no one in this world I'm harder on than myself.

Meggie, my daughter, usually immediately ends this internal debate. Since the day I became a mother at the age of 19, I swore that I would be the mother I never had. I would break the cycle. I wouldn't let my little girl worry about coming home from school and finding her mother dead on the floor or walking into a violent, drunken rage, or worse, a house full of people, partying, doing drugs, or loudly and openly having sex. I was a GenX latchkey kid who truly relished the days when I would come home to an empty house.

However, I must tell you that day on the Courtney Campbell,

I had some pretty convincing arguments why I should. And that's when I knew this was different and this was serious.

That triggering thought awakened a fear and pain in me that I had buried so deeply, I barely recognized it. It didn't roar—it whispered. A familiar ache in an unfamiliar voice.

I sat there at the first light after crossing the 9.9-mile causeway—frozen, hands gripping the wheel tighter than I realized. Memories I thought I had buried deep started rising, clawing their way to the surface. (And trust me—I've seen some shit.)

That was the day I finally understood the Soundgarden words I'd been singing for years: *"I learned that I was a liar."*

That was the day I knew if I was going to try to live, it was time to pull Robin out of my suitcase.

Chapter 2:
Alive

So, I'm still here. Cheers.

I got myself to work. I took a moment in my car to wipe away the tears, breathe, and regroup. I then b-lined to my office, shut the door, and promptly made an online appointment to see a psychiatrist. I didn't pass go. I didn't overthink it.

A psychiatrist. Not Dr. Google, not my family doctor, not my best friends (the West Park Coven), not Reddit, not Vaguebook. A psychiatrist. You know the type of doctors that crazy people like my mother go to. Now, before you come for me for that last statement, just hang with me until you hear my whole story.

Trust that this was perhaps the biggest (only real?) step towards change I've ever taken in my life. And boy have I tried everything. This was rock bottom.

I've spent a literal lifetime chasing the bright and shiny—trying to make it stick. Attending seminars, conferences, and workshops. Collecting certifications (I just earned one in AI last week!). Constantly sharpening the saw of my profession. Reading every book on habits, personality types, time management, and gratitude—quite literally every book. (I did major in English Literature, after all.)

All of it in search of the magic words. The magic cure. The thing that would finally make me into the person I thought I needed to be to be truly happy.

The perfect wife.

The perfect mother.

The perfect daughter.

The perfect executive.

The perfect life I'd always imagined.

I was looking for validation in a world that consistently knocked me down, made me feel small, and kept proving—again—that I was right about myself.

Worthless.

Unlovable.

A failure.

I was convinced, if I could just get it together—reduce my debt, tackle my weight, get organized—You know the New Year's resolution trap. I'd finally be happy. Safe. Secure. Content.

Clearly, I was the problem. All I needed was to just find the roadmap that worked.

I've tried every planner, notebook, system (Covey, EOS, Happy Planner, Bullet Journaling). Nothing worked. Like a needle stuck on a record, no matter how hard I try, I always end up in the same place. Not sticking to it. Sitting on the margins looking in. Never good enough. Not quite. Almost there. Not a real sister, not a real scholar, not in a real career, not in a real marriage, often one paycheck away from losing it all. Waiting for the other shoe to drop.

It was a house of cards I was always strategizing to keep intact, to keep up the façade, to avoid exposure. Taking it all on myself, because the one thing I knew for certain, the only person I could count on was myself. I would never leave me. I could do anything I put my mind to. It was the only thing that I could truly control. The meticulous planner, always one step ahead. Redefining myself. Trying on different roles. Starting something new. Longing for something else.

The ironic thing, I lost myself in my never-ending quest to find myself. *Spoiler alert: I'm the bright and shiny.*

Instead of searching for articles on "how to stop suicidal thoughts" or "how to regain focus," I googled, "online psychiatrists that take insurance in Florida." After all, I need to hide this; no one can know I'm doing this. No one can know that I've gotten this fragile and low.

I have too much responsibility, too many people counting on me, I've got deadlines, an endless to-do list, and a husband with MS and epilepsy. I can't let anyone down—except myself.

So, I need this to fit into my hectic schedule, and it would be better if I didn't have to spend too much money on it because that would alter my debt reduction plan. If I do this online, I can use my lunch hour, and/or in my car on my long commute to/from work, so I'm not home later than I already am. I mean, people depend on me. People rely on me. My husband needs me. My family needs me. The world needs me. Hell, people admire me for my strength.

So, I can't drop the mask. I can't prove them right about me. I can't let them see the real me. I've worked too hard to create this façade. People have expectations of me. And, I already knew, if I didn't live up to those expectations, there were very unpleasant consequences. After all, I'm a GenXer. Proudly raised on hose water and neglect. I'm from the fuck around and find out generation.

"Talksmith" fit the bill.

It was an online service. Check.

I could schedule online. Bonus.

Took my insurance. Excellent.

Could prescribe medication directly to my pharmacy. Check. Check. Check. Check.

Perfect! Let's give it a try, shall we? What have I got to lose?

This last item, "could prescribe medication," was particularly important as I was convinced this needed to be part of the equation. In fact, I thought that might be the missing puzzle piece. I just needed something to help me get through this rough patch.

I was already on a low dose of antidepressants, something I had been on before to handle "situational depression." This was prescribed by my family doctor, and according to her, to several of her other patients in this COVID-19 era. Clearly, Lexapro was no longer doing the trick after four years. *God, has it been four years already?*

Perhaps something like Adderall would help? That might help me regain focus while I get my habits in order, work the 90-day plan, and magically fix it. Something. Anything. The pain was excruciating. Something has got to give.

Something to help me control the chaos so I could get back to living my life. And, by living my life, that meant still having chaos, but in a manner that wouldn't leave me paralyzed to move forward for fear of doing something wrong. That wouldn't have me crying on my bathroom floor or snapping back at people when I was at my breaking point. Something that wouldn't have me binge watching RHOBH in bed all weekend with a "headache."

You know what, I need that sometimes. It's self-care! People are always asking me, "What do you do for self-care?" I tell myself to relieve my guilt.

I was searching for something that wouldn't have me wasting time or starting over again – on Monday, of course. *Love me some procrastination!* Because once I got my health, wealth, and self in order, that would free me up so I can really start living my best life. You know the one where I write that book, try a new career (or job), lose that weight, get my PhD, open the Etsy Shop, perfect hand lettering, start a t-shirt business, live in an orderly house, etc. The one where I finish something. Anything! The one where I no longer had to carry the weight of the world on my shoulders.

The one where vacations aren't spent worrying—

> about my job (Paris),
> the wind and rain (my beach wedding),
> the money being spent (California).

Or my personal favorite: the trip where I had to life-flight my husband from Jamaica to Miami. I lived alone in a hotel for a month, waiting until he was stable enough to travel back to Ohio. Back to the hospital where our neurologist was. Where they knew us. Got us. *Had his fucking chart.*

A place where I didn't have to explain his condition—his symptoms, his history—repeatedly. Don't you people write anything down? Do you read the chart?

A place where I didn't have to recount and relive the trauma just to receive care. Where they would know exactly what to do.

And then—finally—we could go back to our home. Back to our life.

Until the next time this happens.

Alls Well That Ends Well. This too shall pass. Before I know it, I'll be back at my desk and my normal life with another story of survival to tell. *Well done, Sharon.*

This is where my self-deprecating humor and Midwest fast-talking always come in handy. Because of course, people are going to ask me about it. And my job in non-profit requires a lot of small talk. So, I got to have the answers at the ready, so I don't break down, cry, and fall to pieces. Even getting misty-eyed isn't an option for me. *There's no crying in baseball!*

I curate the story and practice the speech until I can deliver it with perfection. Pretending it wasn't that bad. That I'm fine. Most importantly, that I'm grateful that I have the resources that others don't to make it through.

It usually goes something like this:

"OMG. I heard about what happened with Marc. That must have been just awful."

"Yes, it was quite the ordeal," I say with a hint of sarcasm in my voice.

"What happened?" they ask.

I respond, "Well, we were in Jamaica. Marc had a seizure. And when I couldn't wake him up, I called the nurse at our resort. They took us to a hospital via a van-style ambulance. But not the touristy one that only deals with sunburns, food poisoning, and minor breaks and sprains. No, we went to the local hospital. *(Inhale)*

So that was an experience. Let's just say there were goats walking around the compound. Literally, a compound. Armed guards welcomed us at the gate. *(Exhale)*.

But, thankfully, I'm super smart and always prepared. I had trip insurance. I never travel without it, especially when leaving the United States with Marc's health challenges. So soon as I could get him out of there, I did.

Worst 24 hours of my life! But hey, at least I got to ride in a private plane. Check that off the bucket list," I finish.

That usually evokes the laugh I needed to get off this subject. Or the "wow, I don't know how you do it! You're the strongest person I know." *If only they knew. That's not even the half of it.*

"It's nothing," I usually reply, "It's just my life, and I'm used to it."

I then quip, "There is always a silver lining. I'm not a half glass full or half glass empty girl, I'm just glad something is in the glass. Preferably, Champagne."

Mic drop.

I either walk away or smile and say, "Enough about me. How are you?"

Even with those close to me, I don't really go into much more detail. It's self-preservation, really. I just need to put that trauma in the past and move on. Why dwell on it after all? It's just life. And these were the cards I was dealt.

However, at my first family function after the ordeal, I was recounting the tale to my sister Ruthie. She wasn't going to let me off the hook that easily.

Ruthie, a social worker by trade, apparently had talked to Patty, her sister who lives in Ft. Myers. Patty and her husband Jim made the trek across "Alligator Alley" one afternoon to see me and saw first-hand Marc in his postictal state. Something most people don't get the pleasure of seeing.

The postictal state is a period of altered neurological function that occurs after a seizure has ended. It is characterized by a range of symptoms that can vary in severity and duration. The worse the seizure. The worse the postictal state. This one was a doozie.

Marc arrived at the hospital in a medically induced coma. Once he regained consciousness, he had wild hallucinations, paranoia, and extreme combativeness necessitating both leather restraints and a bed sitter. By the time Patty and Jim

17

arrived, he had graduated to soft restraints, and his frame of reality was less distorted. He knew who they were.

He also certainly knew who I was, and my very presence triggered anger. *You know what they say...you hurt the ones you love the most.* While I had been the target of this before, not at this intensity. This time, he was particularly cruel and abusive. Not his fault, of course, but man, this left marks.

And while I did my best to conceal the effect it had on me, Patty and Jim saw enough. They saw behind the mask. They saw the pain. They saw the fear. They saw the exhaustion.

I had been posting daily updates about Marc on our private family Facebook page. It was my way of controlling the narrative and not having to repeat myself a million times. The hospital was already taking care of that. Even though I was doing my best to stick to a routine and project positivity and optimism in these posts, Patty and Jim were able to fill in the blanks between the lines—at least when it came to Ruthie.

Ruthie knew in that moment not to push me too far. A keen observer, she heard my acrylic nails striking the table in anxious rhythm, the pale creeping across my face, and the beads of sweat gathering on my forehead. She lowered her voice and said, "Call me if you want to go for a walk one night (something we regularly did together). I'm guessing you have a little PTSD."

PTSD? What the fuck is she talking about? I didn't just return from war. I just returned from the Caribbean and three weeks in sunny Florida. Although I must admit, when we landed at Hopkins from Miami, I had never been so happy to see the grey skies of Cleveland.

Home at last.

Okay, Talksmith, let's get this party started, shall we?!

This is simple enough. I'm just three steps away from solving this pesky little bridge problem.

1. Fill out the intake form. "We'll ask some basic questions to see if we're a good fit for you." (10 minutes).

2. Based on your needs, we'll match you with a clinician who can help (in less than 12 hours).

3. Self-schedule a virtual visit with the clinician you choose.

I thought to myself, *is this how online dating works?* I wouldn't know. I married my high school sweetheart at 19, pregnant with our daughter, and jumped right into a messy relationship with my current husband who I've been with for 28 years.

I finished the quiz. Got my results.

"Yes, you could use some help," flashed across my screen. *Duh!*

Feeling accomplished, I went about my day of constant triage of people, promises, and problems. The solution to my bridge problem will be in my inbox within the next 12 hours.

Crisis averted. Breathe. Cheers.

Chapter 3:
It's the Most Wonderful Time of the Year

BOOM! AND THERE it was. The unmistakable sound of the leaded glass front door being slammed shut. The sound we'd been anxiously awaiting. The sound that reverberated all the way up to the third floor of the Somerville home, where we lay in wait. The sound that would signal Christmas is here! Finally!

It's hard to believe that someday this same joyous sound of sheer bliss would become the sound of absolute dread. But it did.

On this night, though, it was music to our little ears because what came next was nirvana! The heavenly sound of—"*Santa's Been Here!*"— heralded by the choir of the churchgoers, finally getting back from Christmas Eve Midnight Mass.

This joy, of course, was short-lived.

That signature boom sparked a stampede. One that created a cacophony wrapped in a cyclone of boundless Christmas energy and nervous anticipation. It originated from the very tippy top of the Somerville house—igniting us girls in the 3rd-floor attic dormitory.

We sprinted down the two flights of stairs, picked up the occupant(s) of the cut-through bedroom, and then immediately collided in the hallway with the boys emerging from their second-floor bedroom.

Pushing, shoving, shrieking, and giggling ensued among the throng of us as we all jockeyed for position to be the first down the next two flights of stairs, where all the Somerville Christmas magic awaited.

The Somerville family had two steadfast rules.

1. Everyone had a role in this family, and everyone pitched in. No free rides.

2. Dad worked. Hard. In the steel mills. Mom worked. Hard. In our home. Children listened. Did what was being asked of them. No questions asked. We were expected to be seen, not heard.

Our numerous routines ensured that we always abided by these two rules. Detractors were swiftly punished. Grocery shopping was an Olympic sport, laundry was endless, and dinner time resembled most families' Thanksgiving place settings. It took many hours and many hands to prepare, serve, and clean up meals for our super-sized family.

And, in the Somerville house, the rosary was said as a family every Friday night before anyone went out for the evening... in our chapel.

You heard me. A chapel.

Complete with an altar and a statue of the Virgin Mary.

I mean, when you live in a 1,649-square-foot house with one second-floor bathroom and a locker-sized shower in the creepy basement—shared by thirteen kids—why wouldn't you dedicate an entire room to God?

Boot camp it was not, but we took the house rules seriously. Work hard, play hard—that was the motto. We were a well-oiled machine.

All for one, one for all ... with a healthy appreciation for loopholes. We do like to color outside the lines sometimes.

The Somerville family is old West Park—our neighborhood roots go back multiple generations on both sides. West Park is a historic working-middle-class neighborhood—not a suburb—located in Cleveland. Proper.

It had all the stereotypical trappings of a predominantly Irish Catholic community: lots of firefighters, police officers, and tradesmen. Plenty of bars. Big families. And I mean big.

Six kids were about average. Eight to ten wasn't an anomaly. But the Somervilles...the Somervilles had thirteen children. That made us the largest. Everyone in West Park had at least one Somerville in their grade-school class at OLA—Our Lady of Angels, our family parish.

Our family was so large that neighbors had rules about how many Somervilles were allowed in the yard at one time. Naming all 13 was a neighborhood parlor game –bonus points if you can get them in order. (JoAnne, Jerry, Karen, Donna, Patty, Jack, Ray, Tim, Marian, Ruthie, Annie, Peggy, Marty, and sometimes, Sharon).

The Somervilles talk loud and fast. Laughter is our love language, and whispers are reserved for delivering bad news or talking about a serious subject. We are a party unto ourselves, and our house was always loud and filled with music. (Still Is.)

Our house in West Park was more than four walls. It was our legacy and the heartbeat of our clan. Built by my great-grandfather, Thomas Somerville. Several homes in West Park are a Somerville creation.

My grandfather, Raymond F. Somerville, spent part of his youth in that house before joining the 3-Cs. The 3-Cs—aka the Civilian Conservation Corps (CCC)—were camps established under FDR's New Deal to provide work and relief during the Great Depression. That's where my grandfather first learned the pipefitting trade.

One of my most prized possessions is a sepia-toned photo of my grandfather sitting on the front porch of our family home, looking like the literal poster child for the Depression era. It wasn't until my early twenties that I stopped and thought... *Wait. Do the math.*

If he was just a child in that photo, then he was still a child when he left for the 3-Cs.

I mean, I knew he only had a sixth-grade education—but I'm an English major. I was told there would be no math. *No, really, I was. RIP Dr. Trace.*

No wonder my grandfather was considered a pioneer in the pipefitters' union, fighting for labor rights.

My grandparents, who first met in grade school at OLA and then eventually married in the church there, too, purchased the Somerville family home following World War II with five kids already in tow.

In 1969, my mother, Donna, the fourth oldest of the thirteen Somervilles, brought me, her bastard child, home from the hospital to our family home in West Park, and it is the longest home I have ever lived in.

Christmas Day was the one time a year when routines gave way to tradition in total surrender. It started roughly three days before Christmas. That was the day the tree usually arrived, giving it enough time to drop for Santa to decorate on Christmas Eve.

Wait, Santa doesn't decorate your tree?? We must be special because he always decorates ours.

Special? No. It's pretty genius. I mean, who would want to decorate a Christmas tree with that many kids? Plus, getting it so late in the season meant we could have a gorgeous Blue Spruce on our modest budget and still have plenty of presents underneath it.

I would later parley this Somerville brilliance to fend off my toddler's demands of the neighborhood Ice Cream Truck. A college student and still practically a teenager, I certainly didn't have the money, and I didn't want to disappoint her. I never wanted her to feel left out or different like I did.

So, I convinced Meggie that the "Music Truck" drove around the neighborhood playing music for all the little kids in the neighborhood. Every time she heard the Music Truck come down our street, I interrupted my studies, rose from my desk, and danced with Meggie in front of the living room picture window, as we waved and listened to the Music Truck go by. This ruse lasted until the summer of '93 when Uncle Ray moved in with us following a separation from his wife.

On that day, I was sunbathing on our backyard deck, next to Meggie's kiddie pool, with my college best friend, Tina. We were deep in discussion about Faulkner's *As I Lay Dying*—the book we were reading for the four-week summer Faulkner seminar we were both powering through so that, come fall, my course load would be a little lighter.

Tina and I were both graduate teaching assistants in the English Department at John Carroll University. In addition to being a wife and mother to a toddler, I was a grad student chasing a PhD in Shakespearean studies—because of course, I planned to teach at an Ivy someday. *Spoiler alert: I didn't.*

That semester, I was teaching two sections of freshman composition and a Grammar 101 course—an extra assignment I volunteered for just to bump up my stipend. On top of that, I was studying for my master's exam, outlining my thesis, and juggling a split schedule with my husband. He worked nights so I could go to school during the day, since childcare wasn't in the budget.

He wasn't the only one watching Meggie. Family and friends like Tina helped. But that help came with logistics—drop-offs, pick-ups, and a lot of windshield time. My college was already an hour away, and on any given day, I was crisscrossing the city, coordinating who had her when, and how I was getting from one obligation to the next.

Because he also worked weekends—and, well, needed to sleep at some point—our families stepped in wherever they could. They say it takes a village.

It did. For Meggie. And for me.

I heard the Music Truck in the distance, but skipped our ritual because I knew Meggie was inside, distracted by her two cousins (Ray's kids). And then it happened. Meggie came running outside with her face covered in ninja turtle green frosting. And then with all the childlike excitement at Christmas, she declared.

"Mom! Look at what is in the Music Truck!! ICE CREAM!!!!!!!"

It was like she had just discovered fire, and she was letting me in on the world's greatest secret. I would have loved to share in her joy. But the summer had just started, and now the cat was out of the bag. I don't need this shit. Haven't I got enough to deal with?

Instead, I asked, "Who bought you that?"

Meggie replied, "Uncle Ray."

"Of course, he did," I uttered under my breath as I marched into the house. Honestly, there were no other suspects.

I found Ray and said, "From this day forward, when my kid wants Ice Cream from the Music Truck. You will buy it for her every single time. I don't care if it's 2-3x a day (again, summer, that is how many times they passed in a day), I will never dry the tears of my kid over ice cream."

This was said in my signature voice that signals - I ain't fuckin' around here! This is something a lot of people in my life have mistaken for yelling. Trust me, you will know when I'm yelling.

Not waiting for any reply or discussion, I promptly turned

around and went back to my sunbathing and discussing the Bundren family, knowing that the problem was solved. Next.

The Somerville family Christmas tree took up residency in the chapel. The chapel was the sunporch—aka the Florida Room—located off the dining room behind a set of cherry wood French doors. Our dining room, however, functioned as the TV/family room.

We didn't need a dining room. My grandparents weren't exactly throwing dinner parties. Instead, we had an industrial U-shaped breakfast nook in the kitchen, built by my grandfather's hands, with a table large enough to seat our regular party of ten-plus and sturdy enough to withstand our ruckus. The Somervilles are not exactly a gentle bunch.

We piled in and arranged ourselves by age. The youngest always sat in the back, while the rest fanned out from the center like a rainbow. And if any of us younger kids needed out at any point during dinner, we had to crawl under the table like a canary in a coal mine.

The only time I ever made it close to the front was on my birthday. That was your reward—moving to the head of the table for cake and the terribly off-tune Somerville choir singing "Happy Birthday," complete with cha-cha-chas and a refrain of "May the Dear Lord Bless You."

To this day, it's why I refuse to scoot into a booth. I always ask for a table at a restaurant over a booth.

Nope. Done. I did my time.

When we finally reached the bottom of the stairs, what awaited us was something truly magical. The Miracle on Allien Ave. It was like we just walked into the downtown department store at Christmas time.

For us, that would be Higbee's – Cleveland's version of Macy's, and where the movie *A Christmas Story* was filmed. The infamous leg lamp, which has become a decorative Christmas staple, was first illuminated in a home in Tremont, another neighborhood of Cleveland. Proper. *Fun fact. Tremont is also where celebrity Chef Michael Symon opened his first restaurant, Lola.*

As depicted in the movie, Cleveland families made an annual pilgrimage downtown, dressed in their finest, to see Santa, visit Mr. Jingling's shop, and if you were lucky, have lunch at the Silver Grille. Higbee's fancy restaurant was modeled after the Blue Box at Tiffany's.

Remember, this was long before you could go to your local mall to see Santa. Sure, we had strip malls and some of them were anchored with larger stores like Sears or JCPenney, but all the department stores were in downtown Cleveland.

Somehow, my family managed to recreate this exact department store look, feel, and warmth on this one magical day of the year.

Although there were signs of Christmas in the house starting after the only family December birthday on the 10th, the Christmas magic didn't really come alive until Santa Claus finished all the lights and tree decorations. The frosting and sprinkles on the cake, in other words. *Who doesn't love cake?*

Until then, Christmas cards were taped inside the square grids of the French doors, the melted-plastic popcorn Santa hung proudly on the front door, and the Hummel nativity—sans wise men, of course—was displayed on the built-ins flanking the fireplace.

Except these weren't ordinary built-ins. They were part of a high-fidelity custom stereo system, one of those sleek wall units where the speakers and components were seamlessly tucked into the custom oak cabinetry around the hearth.

As you can imagine, with a family of our size, lots of things got broken over the years, especially kitchen glassware. Something we apparently never outgrew. My husband officially banned any glassware being used when we were entertaining my side of the family. In 2014, my cousin Rachel received a surprise bill in the mail following her wedding for "the excessive number of broken glasses." She didn't even bother to dispute it and promptly remitted payment.

But the few precious family heirlooms—my great-grand-mother's Madonna and Child Hummel with its authentic German stamp, her Royal Doulton serving platter, the German beer steins with their pewter lids, and the Goebel Friar Tuck salt-and-pepper shakers—were proudly displayed atop those built-ins, not tucked away in some protective China cabinet.

The Friar Tucks came from my grandparents' only trip to Europe, financed by winnings from a Super Bowl football pool at the pipefitters' union hall.

"Ruth, pack your bags—we're going to see the Pope," my grandfather declared.

Somehow, all of it survived the chaos of our rowdy household.

However, my grandmother's "good China"—the set she'd painstakingly collected piece by piece with redeemed S&H Green Stamps—did not.

Man, I loved putting those stamps in the book. No wonder I'm such a sticker freak.

When we came down from "bed" on Christmas Eve, there were what felt like hundreds of presents everywhere—starting in the living room at the bottom of the stairs, which ran the length of the front of the house, through the TV room at the rear, and spilling into and around the perimeter walls of the chapel. Everything was neatly stacked in piles. Finding yours was akin to searching for your Easter basket.

Honestly, looking back, no wonder I thought it was magic.

Just the amount of wrapping paper alone required a small workforce. The time it must have taken to wrap all those presents. Impressive.

Christmas was a full production. But like everything else in the Somerville house, there was a system. And once you aged out of believing in Santa, you became part of it. You didn't even think about ruining it for the believers—if for no other reason than because you still longed for that feeling.

To this day, the Somerville family still gathers and opens presents on Christmas Eve.

Our systems incorporated a bit of a fairness as well. Each child got five basic things:

1. **Something you want a.k.a. The Santa Request.** This was the gift you were going to ask Santa for when you sat on his lap at Higbee's. We would spend hours upon hours paging through the Sears catalogue identifying that *one gift*. If you chose something out of the family price range, Santa's choice. Sorry for the disappointment kids, but that is how life works. *But a girl can dream, can't she?*

2. **Something you need.** Usually a winter coat, boots, or socks in the lean years. You would provide "hints" on your Christmas List on what you wanted it to look like.

3. **Something to wear.** Usually a sweater. Not a Christmas sweater but something new with the tags on that no one else has ever worn. Hand-me-downs and thrift store shopping were a necessity in a family our size. *Probably not a coincidence that I spent nearly a decade fundraising for an organization called Shoes and Clothes for Kids whose tagline is More than new outfits. New outlooks.*

4. **Something to listen to.** We all got a record for the Hi-Fi system. Usually, a two-song A/B side 45. If you got a full-length album, either it was your Santa Request, or there was a lot of overtime that year. We patiently waited our turn to spin the black circle. We went in age order, of course, so I usually didn't get my turn until Christmas Day. Needless to say, I associate every one of my family members with a specific record or artist.

5. **Something that most families would find in their stockings.** Our mantle was adorned with actual socks from the mismatch pile and were filled with a variety of candy, including one candy cane, and a piece of fruit to take up most of the stocking. So, for Christmas we would get a "small" stocking stuffer style gift like a Christmas Ornament, a Diary, Coloring Books, etc.

There was always a "family gift" from Santa as well. Once we were done opening all our gifts, the family gift was revealed. This was never a trip to Disney World, but that homemade ice-cream maker we got the one year, was just as exciting. It is also the reason I was adamant I would never let my child cry over ice cream.

But there was one Christmas when the rules changed. When the family gift wasn't for all of us. When it was for me.

The year my mother was in the hospital (4C), the big reveal was actually for me! A big girl bike was wheeled in the back door into the kitchen for me!

This wasn't just any bike. It was the pink Schwinn banana seat bike with a sissy bar and training wheels, complete with a bell, daisy-adorned plastic basket, and handlebar streamers! Just like the one in the catalogue!

This wasn't even my Santa wish! My wish that year was that my mom could come home...but this was right up there! I felt like *something special.*

I already knew I wasn't going to get my Santa wish, *but close*. They were going to let her out of the psychiatric ward, briefly, for Christmas dinner. She would need to return because she wasn't quite well enough to come home – aka – take care of me. My grandparents "committed her" after an attempt to take her life by swallowing a bottle of pills and washing it down with a bottle of vodka. My grandparents told me that I would need to be a brave girl for a little longer.

My mom was quite subdued (medicated) for that visit. She cried a lot, and they weren't happy tears. I could tell she was "sick." She did bring me a present, though. A green octopus she made from yarn.

It was better than the bike.

As flawed as it was, this would be my last happy childhood Somerville Christmas Eve. This would be my last Christmas with my grandfather and the second last Christmas with my grandmother.

My grandfather suffered his second stroke a few days after Christmas and died on February 13, 1977. My grandmother was diagnosed with cancer that November and died on April 5, 1978. They were both 57 at the time of their deaths.

Every Christmas that followed, until I was an adult, involved some sort of trauma—not drama, like most families.

Chapter 4:
The Old Man and the Sea

RECALLING MY CHILDHOOD is difficult, painful, and honestly, quite a blur. Trauma will do that to you, I guess. As a result, I've often questioned if things I recall are true or just a story I made up for myself, about myself, so I can live with myself. Am I just pretending that life with my grandparents was all puppies, kitties, and rainbows, or is it veneration of the dead, or nostalgia? Am I gaslighting myself? I mean, I do have quite a few people to corroborate things like our Christmas Eve traditions, but their perspective and perception will always be different than mine. What gives their version more validity than mine? Aren't we all just the unreliable narrators of all our own tales?

I do have physical scars from childhood accidents, above my right eyebrow and on my left middle finger. I do have photos. There is a picture of me in my Batman costume, on Christmas Eve, not Halloween, sitting on a living room couch surrounded by my cousins, wearing those same Mary Jane shoes and white socks I recall so vividly. I'm looking oh so pensive, like the weight of the world was on my shoulders. (It was).

But other things are met with "I don't think that is how that happened."

Case in point. A core memory and story I've told a million times over about how I came to read, write and acquire a rather large vocabulary by the time I was barely four. This was highly unusual in the early 70s. You weren't expected to come to school with knowledge, you went to school to gain knowledge.

As an astute student of the world around me, I absolutely couldn't wait to start school and learn new things. Another venture I took off for solo. I wouldn't even let anyone walk me to school. Fiercely independent.

Kindergarten look-out. I came to slay. *Oh, the places you'll go!*

So, imagine my frustration when I realized that our half-day kindergarten was nothing more than a play-based curriculum that even included naptime. Now, I'm all for naptime. Team Nap for Life. But this was not what I signed up for.

These kids couldn't even write their own first and last name, let alone read. I wasn't here to learn my ABCs or draw pictures, I was ready to go. I had a lot to do. Survival wasn't easy in my world, and this Batman could use a few more tools in her belt.

It's not that I was a prodigy. Sure, I was smart, sharp, and observant, but my premature knowledge is the result of a rather endearing story. One that starts with my grand-father, Raymond F. Somerville, who had only a sixth-grade education, and intersects with Ernest Hemingway, winner of both the Pulitzer and Nobel prizes for Literature. Champagne and Hashbrowns...*And so it goes.*

> My grandfather had his first stroke shortly following my second birthday. Now, naturally, being his first granddaughter and living under his roof, I was the apple of his eye. So, we were already besties.

> While most of the kids sat on the floor, I was the one who got to sit on his lap on Sunday nights while the family gathered around the 25-inch Zenith Chroma color console TV to watch the *Wonderful World of Disney.*

> I alone enjoyed his spearmint leaf jelly-candy that were strictly off limits. One, because they were HIS, just like his stereotypical Archie Bunker 70s yellow plaid dad's chair that you didn't dare sit in, even when he

wasn't around. Two, we had a hard and fast rule: no food outside the kitchen. *Ask me about the Spaghetti Incident sometime.*

As a result of his stroke, he lost the ability to speak, read, write, and had extensive damage to his motor skills. This meant that he couldn't work for quite some time as he rehabilitated. And, trust me, there was no speech, physical, or occupational therapy coming to the house.

My grandfather was a bearish man, with a distinctive, deep-dimpled cleft chin with piercing green eyes. He was not only intimidating—he was also kind of a badass. A Navy Seabee during World War II, he was stationed in the Philippines. Seabees were known for their "Can Do" motto. They built bases and airfields, roads and infrastructure. Highly skilled tradesmen. The ones who got shit done.

Hmm. That explains a few things about me.

Because my grandpa was a proud man, having to learn to speak and read all over again was deeply unwelcome. He didn't attempt to converse with many people— mostly out of embarrassment. And when he did, true to a sailor, his words were often laced with curse words born of frustration.

We often joke that in our family; *fuck* is among the first words you'll hear. It's so normalized you'll rarely hear "language—not in front of the kids." It's the language of sailors and tradesmen, passed down like everything else in our family. Half the time, I don't even hear it coming out of my own mouth.

But, since I was a child learning all about this world around me, I wouldn't know if he was stuttering, using the wrong words, or heck, even cursing.

We spent a lot of time together at a time I was soaking everything up like a sponge. My mom was at work, kids were at school, and my gram was busy running our enormous household. It was just me and him. We were in this together.

While I don't recall any actual "lessons," I do know that during this time my grandfather taught me how to fish. We'd either head down to the creek in the Metroparks behind our house or ride out to the Rocky River fishing pier on Lake Erie—which, to me, looked like the ocean, complete with a small beach.

While we fished, my grandfather would read aloud to me as part of his rehabilitation. Ernest Hemingway's *The Old Man and the Sea.*

It was there—sitting beside him, rod in hand—that I fell in love with literature. With stories. With the idea of becoming a writer. The book made me fall in love with Florida, too—with its themes of resilience, resistance, and caring for others even when your own strength is failing. It remains one of my all-time favorite books.

Looking back, it's impossible not to see us in those pages.

Just like Santiago and the boy.

To this day, every year on February 13th, the anniversary of my grandfather's death, I re-read *The Old Man and the Sea* in his honor.

Awe...

That is the story I tell. That is the story that anchors me. That is the story that evokes a warm, comforting, safe feeling of love. That, my friend, however, is a story that raises all kinds of red flags.

Is this a Hallmark movie?

For starters, I highly doubt my grandfather read me *The Old Man and the Sea*. I mean I know I did read *my* daughter, *Othello* as a child...but as his oldest daughter once commented, "What? My Dad never read a book in his life. Let alone Ernest Hemingway. Comical."

Reactions like that would eventually have a profound effect on me. Over time, being criticized became my kryptonite—soul-crushing in its precision. Remember: I am flawed, unworthy, an outsider, a bastard. So, questioning my authority, memory, or validity only fuels that narrative.

I replay those conversations repeatedly in my head, dissecting every word until I've performed a full emotional autopsy. Then, once I've exhausted myself, I turn to the one thing I know how to do best: I become an expert in whatever made me feel small. It's my way of fighting back. In other words, I do what I'm wired to do—I intellect.

As a child, I carried around an index card and wrote down every word or phrase I didn't understand, so I could look it up later at the library. In the age of the internet, I mastered the art of early search engines, AltaVista, Lycos, and Excite. An early career bio noted that I could "find anything on the internet in under 10 seconds flat!" It became a valuable asset in my nonprofit work in the small shops I worked, as we didn't have the funds for prospecting or wealth screening tools.

But, in the age of instant gratification and Google, it became dangerous. That same curiosity has sent me down more internet rabbit holes than I can count. My love of problem solving and quest for knowledge turned into obsession (*true crime anyone)* and became rocket fuel my procrastination, self-diagnosis, self-doubt, self-sabotage, self-loathing—especially during the pandemic when we were all on high-alert.

So, while this Hallmark version might not be the exact way this story happened, some of it must be true. I didn't just decide to one day love Ernest Hemingway. I don't think it's any coincidence that when you walk into my house, one of the first things you will see a carved wooden mask with a Marlin that we bought on our wedding day in Jamaica.

Yes, my diva husband had to stop and shop in the middle of taking our wedding pictures. Like me, he's attracted to the bright and shiny. There was a makeshift "street fair" in the town square of our resort. I immediately saw it as a sign from a guardian angel. Marc, recognizing this in me, asked if they could carve our wedding date on it. They could and we'd swing back by on the way to our beach "reception."

You can also find several pieces of Guy Harvey's artwork throughout our home: in our bathrooms, dining room, over the fishtank, on throw pillows, and of course, in the kitchen.

I did go on to major in English literature, buy a home on Lake Erie—with a view from every room—move to Florida, visit Hemingway's home, corner bar, and writing room in Key West with my own two eyes. Like him, I walked the streets of Paris and wrote a book.

Unlike, him, however, I also stopped myself—and sought immediate help—the day I thought about driving off a bridge.

This story might not have happened that way, but it is my north star or rather, my second star to the right. It is the one sentence that is true.

Hemingway once wrote: "I would stand and look out over the roofs in Paris and think, 'Do not worry. You have always written and you will write now. All you have to do is write one true sentence. Write the truest sentence you know.' So, I would finally write that one true sentence and then go on from there. It was easy then because there was always one true sentence that you know or had seen or had heard someone say."

This I know is true: Learning to navigate the world together was an experience only I had with my grandfather. It was a gift that profoundly shaped me, especially since I had no father. When we made Father's Day gifts at school I made them for him. Same with Christmas gifts. I made him a ceramic Mickey Mouse in a stocking that is so fragile now, I can no longer risk it falling off the tree for fear that it will finally break beyond repair.

This I know is true: Like Hemingway, my grandfather was flawed. A drunk, abuser, and emotionally absent father. This is not the relationship or memories I have of him. Mine stop on Christmas Eve 1976. But I have heard the stories. He may have caused trauma in our family but not for me. *Except that dying thing.*

This I know is true: My grandfather strongly resembled Hemingway. He was stout, balding, and his limited pictures include life experiences of being on vacation with his wife, serving in World War II, snapshots of holidays, and getting dressed up on the way to a wake/funeral —because nothing says date night like an Irish wake in West Park. There is also the picture of my proud Papa Somerville sitting at the Public House, our corner bar, the day I was born.

This I know is true: He was with me the day I tried to live. Don't believe me? Have you ever driven to the Keys? Or heck even Put-In-Bay, it's a series of bridges over water.

The story of my grandfather feels like the beginning of everything, but really it was just the setup. Before the sea came the storm—the night I was born in the middle of a Cleveland blizzard.

Chapter 5:
But I Wanted a Football

"I had a brother
But now my brother is gone"
— Eddie Vedder, "Brother the Cloud"

I WAS BORN ON Saturday night during a snowstorm in January 1969 at 9:53 p.m. My mother was twenty-two years old and an unwed, single mother by "choice." Ironically, this was during a time when women didn't really have a "choice." **Roe v. Wade** wouldn't be decided until 1973. It was the era of the shotgun wedding. Her pregnancy brought great shame on our big Catholic family.

My father, Mr. Blankspace, as my mother tells it, claims she told him that if he couldn't be a full-time father, then he shouldn't be my father at all. She didn't want me waiting on the doorstep for him to show up for weekly visits, only to see the disappointment in my eyes when he didn't. Apparently, he knew he wouldn't live up to his part of the bargain.

So, he chose to walk away. Just like that.

His actual name is not on my birth certificate because in 1969 unwed mothers were prohibited from listing a father's name on a birth certificate unless he signed an acknowledgment of paternity, as it legally bound him.

Now, we've never met but my mad investigative skills and insatiable curiosity allowed me to keep tabs on him. First via the annual telephone book. Each year, when the white pages showed up on our doorstep, I would immediately turn to the

D's. Scanned for his last name, which is distinct and has a unique spelling, just like Somerville with an O and one M.

And there it was every year, his mother's name, address and telephone number. I never called it. I just liked knowing I could. After all, it was not my responsibility to find him, he's the one that left me. Plus, that would spoil my childhood princess rescue fantasy.

The internet gave me greater access to photos, newspaper articles, yearbook. property records, phone numbers Then, in my forties, at my daughter's behest, I wrote him a letter. Because of course, I did, I'm a writer! My young scientist had urged me to if for no other reason than to understand what might be lurking in the gene pool.

Mr. Blankspace and I have spoken twice—and I've had warmer conversations with bill collectors. There's no relationship, no curiosity, no acknowledgment that I even exist. I honestly don't know if he ever really knew he had a daughter. He didn't even remember my mother's name.

But I do know this: he's never known me. The daughter who grew up to be strong, complicated, a little scarred, and kind of extraordinary. The daughter who learned to rise above the hand that held her down.

I can think. I can reason. I can write and love and imagine. I can hold my own, and I can survive things that would have folded a lesser spirit. I've done it more than once.

And sometimes I wonder—if he hadn't walked away, would I still be this woman? Would I still have this grit, this empathy, this drive to make meaning out of the mess?

So maybe, in the end, he didn't really miss a thing.

It might seem like a noble choice—my mother protecting her child—but considering that she loved to tell the story of how drunk she was on New Year's Eve, just twelve days before my birth, I don't think so.

This is not a Hallmark story. And it's not even really a Lifetime story.

Whatever the case, consequently, I became a Somerville through and through. I was brought home to my grandparents' house, and they took charge of my care. They knew their unwed daughter—who brought great shame to our Catholic home—have I mentioned the shame? couldn't adequately care for me on her own. They stepped in without hesitation.

The younger kids—Marian, Ruthie, Annie, Peggy, and Marty— embraced me as their "sister," and before long, I just sort of became the 14th Somerville.

A few of the older kids were still in the house, too. Ray, a senior in high school, kicked off my love of football. A star on the Cathedral Latin football team, my mom attended every game while she was pregnant with me. At least I had some positive in utero experiences.

Marian and Ruthie, also both in high school, greeted me each day like a child they were there to babysit. Annie and Peggy, the two youngest girls, as I would learn years later, harbored jealousy toward me for the attention I received—especially from their father.

And then there was Marty. The youngest. A kindergartener. Number thirteen. Only six years older than me on the day I was born—and from that day, my kindred spirit.

When Marty was born, my mother, the fourth oldest, was the oldest girl still living at home. The two older girls had left the nest to join the convent. A Catholic family's wet dream.

Marty and my mother shared a deep bond; she always treated him as someone special. She was sixteen when he was born and, like Marian and Ruthie would later do with me, she made sure he was fed, had fresh diapers, and clean clothes.

The difference was my mom wasn't a student; she was a working girl. No, not that kind! Instead of attending high school after eighth grade, she chose "beauty school," as they called it back then, and became a teenage cosmetologist. She earned good money for her age and with that money, she doted on Marty and the younger kids—showering them with gifts, buying them clothes, shoes, soda, candy, and toys—luxuries outside of holidays in a family our size.

Somehow, my mother managed to hide her pregnancy from the family until she was eight months along. The large smocks she wore for work and her fuller figure allowed her to conceal her growing belly. She also wore a girdle with boning every day. (There weren't Spanx last century.) I was born with my forehead smashed in.

When she finally told the family, she told Marty she was bringing him home a "big surprise."

As he used to tell the story, he thought I was going to be a new football—but instead, he got me. I'm sure he was initially disappointed, but little did he know, I would turn out to be one of the best gifts he'd ever been given.

Unlike my father, Marty chose to unwrap it, embrace it, love it unconditionally, play with it, and nurture it until the day he died—October 27, 1997. I was 28, and he was 35.

Prior to Marty's death, every single significant and insignificant moment of my life was shared with him.

First, the insignificant ones. In our large family, it was understood that the older kids looked after the younger ones. Even though Marty had been the baby for almost seven years, when I came along, he, too, despite his young age, was charged with looking after me. He was no longer the baby—I was.

So, every time I came home crying because of skinned knees, someone being mean to me, or losing at kick-the-can (girls do cry over that)—Marty got in trouble for not watching me closely enough.

Of course, there were bigger incidents—kids will be kids—like the time he dared me to put my hand in the flywheel of the exercise bike as he operated the pedals "watch this, Sha." (Sha is my family nickname, pronounced Shea, like the stadium.)

It didn't end well.

My left middle finger was so badly chewed up that all they could do was let it heal into the lumpy scar I still bear to this day. I think that might be why eventually he made sure I had a big ole diamond engagement ring, so that you noticed that instead of my scar.

Sadly, Marty was the one who was punished for those things—often physically—but he never held it against me. Not once.

Throughout my life, he was always my biggest cheerleader. He cheered the loudest at my grade-school graduation when I received the Benny Bonanno Resolution, and again, at my high school graduation. He sobbed with pride the day I graduated top of my English class at John Carroll University.

I would have never graduated at all if it wasn't for Marty. He provided me the safety and security to have the courage to take on becoming a mother at 19.

When I found myself unexpectedly pregnant my freshman year of college. I got married—I think I mentioned the shame already. I had a full-blown 250+ guest wedding to my boyfriend of two years.

The waterfront engagement party was at Shooters on the River, in Cleveland's infamous Flats, planned and paid for by Marty, of course. We even picked out my engagement ring together. He had a connection to a jewelry purchaser for Tiffany & Co., which meant I ended up with a sparkler well beyond what most of the 19-year-old kids could afford. My family later used this connection and chipped in for set of cultured pearls with a pink hue when I graduated college. *A lady should always have a strand of pearls.*

The wedding came together in just eight weeks—another clue I was destined to be an event planner. I had a plan, a timeline, and a mission to make it happen.

I had the princess wedding of my dreams. Ray bought my wedding dress, and the bridesmaids' dresses were upcycled from my best friend, Heather's, sister's recent wedding. The favors were also custom-made. The union hall caterer, of course, could handle a Somerville wedding on short notice.

Plus, I still managed to get a semester of college in before the baby came. Marty made sure that.

Once I make up my mind about something, I find a way to make it happen. I was learning that life's detours could be overcome—one timeline at a time. "Trust the timing of your life" my grandmother would always say.

But that wasn't courage, not yet. It was survival. A blip. A small sacrifice for safety. I built a smaller life because smaller felt safe.

And then Marty died.

I could spend the rest of this book telling just stories about Marty. His loss was a profound one for every member of our family and anyone who knew him. *And I mean anyone.* He was the brightest light in the universe. Hilarious. Wild. Impulsive.

Cursed with the Somerville fat gene, Marty never apologized for it. He could've doubled for Chris Farley in the SNL Chippendales audition sketch—same fearless abandon, same absolute commitment to the bit.

I'm fairly certain that at some point during my wedding, shirts were abandoned entirely, chest hair on full display, joy uncontained. Talk about dancing like no one is watching.

Mention you're thinking about remodeling your kitchen? Marty helps himself to your garage—sledgehammer already in hand.

"Let's get this party started," he declares as he takes his first strike. Before you even have time to protest. No changing your mind now. No worries. A pipefitter like his dad and brothers, Marty knew exactly how to spot a load-bearing wall.

Allow him to take your car up to family camping spot in the Allegany mountains three hours away...*as long as he has someone in the car with a valid license.*

Marty brings Sonny, our yellow labrador retriever, named after our favorite pizza joint.

"You didn't specify what kind of license," he would argue.

Okay, just one more.

The Somervilles are a football family. And since we're from Cleveland, we were born into loving the most dysfunctional, luckless, heartbreaking franchise in the NFL. Nonetheless, we show up every Sunday, tailgate like there is no kickoff, and relish in the fact that there is always next year.

My 18th birthday was the first time the Cleveland Browns ever came close to going to the Super Bowl. This was 1987—no online ticketing for us. All I wanted for my birthday was the hottest ticket in town. So, to make my birthday wish come true, my brother Marty and cousin Michael spent the overnight outside of Cleveland Municipal Stadium in January while Lake Erie fired up its snow machine and produced winds resulting in sub-zero temperatures. Now that is love. 💜

And yes, my friends, that game was also known as The Drive. Being a Cleveland Browns sports fan should qualify as its own trauma category.

Marty's death broke me in places I didn't even realize I could be broken. And I remained broken for so many years. I look back now and think of all that wasted light, but then I remember, it's all part of my journey.

For a long time, I didn't think I'd ever get up from that kind of pain. But broken doesn't mean finished. I didn't know it then, but the cracks were where the light would eventually start to get in.

Marty's voice—his laugh, his chaos, his way of making ordinary days feel like events—became the echo that kept me moving. And I swear, sometimes when life gets loud and messy and I'm not sure I can do it, I still hear him: "C'mon, Sha. You got this."

That voice was with me when I ran my first 10K—the inaugural Sunshine Skyway Run, where runners raise money for military families as they tackle a roadway many people refuse, or are too frightened, to cross even by car.

He was with me that day on the Courtney Campbell Causeway, too.

I met Marc the summer before Marty died. They never met, but my last conversation with Marty was about him. I told Marty about this guy—kind, funny, grounded, dashingly handsome, and with a fashion sense that could rival mine. Someone who, like me, loved to live life out loud.

The timing was terrible. There were other lives already in motion, other hearts that would be smashed by what followed. I wish it had unfolded differently. I carry the weight of that choice—quietly, and still.

Hearts don't break cleanly, and mine was already in pieces. But even in the middle of the chaos, I knew Marc's presence in my life wasn't accidental. I still believe the universe sends people exactly when we need them most. For me, that was Marc. From the start, it felt like Marty had a hand in it—like he wasn't really gone, just rearranging things from wherever he landed next.

Marc would become the bridge between who I was and who I was still becoming.

Marc was my own personal rockstar.

Part 2:
Pretty on the Outside

The Shiny Life

Chapter 6:
Waiting for Stevie

*"You can be loved by everyone
And still not feel, not feel loved"
—Pearl Jam, "Waiting for Stevie"*

I ALWAYS KNEW I wanted a big life. Of course, what that life looked like over the years has changed. But I always knew I wanted to see and experience the whole wide world. All those amazing places I read about in books, magazines, and Encyclopedia Britannica—now Wikipedia. I wanted to see them for myself and make memories there, instead of vicariously living through characters, actors, and stories.

I love the princess narrative as much as I love Champagne and Hashbrowns. After all, I was a damsel in distress, waiting for my father to come rescue me so we could live happily ever after. And even when I realized—fuck that shit, I'm going to rescue myself—I still carried the weight, shame, and resentment for years that he didn't. I also knew I wanted to be a trailblazer—like Jo Marsh.

Louisa May Alcott's *Little Women*, published in 1868, over 100 years before I was born, was the first real "adult novel" I ever read. The four Marsh sisters—Meg, Jo, Beth, and Amy—navigate sisterhood, grief, and ambition during the Civil War, with their beloved Marmie (mom) guiding them. And Laurie? He was the original "boy next door" who understood the girls better than most men ever would.

But writer Jo? She was my girl. Fiercely independent, wildly creative, quick to anger, and stubborn as hell. Like me, she would rather figure it out on her own than ask for help. (Selling her hair instead of asking her wealthy Aunt for train money for Marmie to visit her wounded father).

Jo was considered clever. She pushed the boundaries but was also acutely aware of a woman's place in the "real world." It was acceptable to ask questions and demand answers—right up to the point where someone reminded you of the glass ceiling. Or worse, that if you didn't fit the mold or spoke out of turn, there would be consequences.

Some of those consequences were serious. Losing your job, for instance. Even when you were 100 percent right. Even when the *I told you so* was coming so hard you'd bet your house on it. This is where a big mouth and boldness can get you into trouble.

See—my mom was right. She used to say, "Sharon, one day your big mouth is going to get you in trouble."

She wasn't wrong.

No one was safe from my sharp tongue. I collected monikers like brat, bitch, sassy, difficult, bold, overpowering, smart ass, cold-hearted, aloof—wearing them with pride. This is who I am. Take it or leave it. I'm not everyone's cup of tea, which is just fine, because I drink coffee.

That was the outward me.

The part people don't see is that the loudest voices often belong to the people with the busiest minds and the biggest hearts. Creative brains. Empaths. Caretakers. The ones who overthink everything but still show up with an I am who I am posture because they must. Because anything less feels like disappearing.

And while we may look put together, it's a performance. We care what people think. We feel too much. We think too much. We hurt.

At least I did.

Characters like Jo validated that.

Naturally, I became immediately obsessed with the story and characters. This led to my first collection of *pretty things*. It was The Madam Alexander *Little Women* doll collection, which included both Marmie and Laurie!

These dolls weren't playthings.

They came in beautiful cornflower blue cardboard boxes with the words "Madame (green) Alexander (pink)" interlaced in a crisscross pattern. These script "X" s were adored with fuchsia poppy flowers. When you lifted off the box top, folded pink tissue paper invited you to reveal the doll inside. The only thing that would have made it more exciting would have been a satin ribbon tied around the box.

It took a few occasions to complete my collection—most of which was bought for me by my widowed grandmother. Since my birthday was just a few weeks after Christmas, I assembled the girls quickly. On Valentine's Day, I received Marmie, and then Laurie for Easter. The last day I would see her alive.

I displayed and cared for that collection like they were Fabergé eggs. I would hand-launder and iron their clothes, keep them on stands, and dust them with care. It was my most cherished collection.

These dolls offered me the same comfort Robin once had, but this time, their beauty was meant to be seen. It was a small but certain step toward showing the world who I was—a girl who loved things that sparkled, things that told stories, things that made life just a little more beautiful.

When my grandmother died just 14 short months after my grandfather, my mother's coworker bought me a Barbie fur coat. When I opened it, I was like thanks, but I don't have any Barbies. She said "hmm. Your mom said you loved playing with your dolls; I guess I just thought Barbie."

Well, you thought wrong!

But God bless her, this is how I got introduced to the wonderful world of Barbie.

The Marsh sisters' story was already written. Barbie could be anything. And here started my obsession with shoes, clothing and trying on different careers.

No doubt Barbie contributed to my sense of ideal body images—along with Kate Moss—but just like Disney taught me, if you can believe it, you can achieve it. I tended to focus on the fact that Barbie had her own dream house, camper, a corvette and a Jeep, and was a doctor, stewardess, and Olympic athlete. She had a career. She did this all on her own. She could bring home the bacon and fry it up in a pan. Ken was just arm candy. The trophy husband. Who needs a prince?

So, having said all that, imagine this scene: 5th grade, Sr. Leo's class at OLA. She was the meanest, most intimidating nun I've ever met. The Nurse Ratchet of her convent, indeed.

We were asked to stand up in front of the class and espouse our hopes and dreams for the future.

A determined young lady, I confidently stood up and proclaimed that I was either going to be the first woman Supreme Court Justice (there wasn't one at the time) or the first woman President of the United States (there still isn't one... so I still have a shot).

I had big dreams—an Ivy League law degree, followed by a famous, successful career.

Sr. Leo, of course, scoffed at my ambitions, made a few derogatory comments about my family—whom she had schooled for years—and sent a foolish girl back to her seat.

I returned to my seat discouraged but not defeated. Instead of being crushed, I set a course to achieve greatness.

That was the start of my "oh yeah, I'll show you!" attitude, which was conveniently coupled with the voice inside my head that heard that nun say: *"Silly girl, you can't be President or on the Supreme Court. Not only are you a woman, but you have your mother's last name. And I've been teaching Somervilles for a while, and if you're anything like Marty, Annie, Peggy, or Ruthie—good luck! Plus, you don't have that kind of money."*

In all fairness to Sr. Leo, my mother did stop her education after 8th grade, and I was among the first in my family to graduate from college. But still...

Now, I realize those were probably not my exact words—nor did I have the financial acumen to worry about how I was going to pay for it—but I do know that's how that core memory makes me feel. And I spent the better part of my life with that demonic angel on my shoulder, chirping in my ear, as I feverishly tried to defeat the odds.

Juxtaposed against this fire in my belly was a home life spinning out of control. After my grandparents died, my mother's drinking worsened, and I spent a short time living alone with her before moving back to the house on Allien Avenue—the only place that still felt like home.

Allien was the one place that confirmed me, where I felt safe, where I belonged. I was no longer the illegitimate child drifting from place to place with her single mom, starting over at new schools and explaining, repeatedly, that I didn't have a dad.

No, I've never seen him. No, I've never met him. (Still haven't, to this day.)

Plus, I would have witnesses to her violent outbursts, the crying, the apologies, and gifts that followed. They would now see the constant eggshells I walked on. I could also return to OLA, the friends I had made in the neighborhood, my sisters, Ruthie, Annie, Peggy and my protector Marty.

That was short lived. Peggy soon graduated from high school and moved to Ft. Myers, FL to attend college. Annie met Rick and moved in with him, eventually relocating to the Upper Peninsula of Xichigan. Ruthie moved to Alabama to live with

Joanne. Marty went to live with Jerry because Marty was a minor and Jerry was the executor of the Somerville estate. My refuge quickly turned into a house of horrors and a lifestyle that would follow me up until my high school graduation.

Instead of having that familial life I longed for, I basically lived in a frat house. When I wasn't in school or at the library, I was left in the house alone while mom worked at the salon by day, and then the neighborhood bar our family owned, by night.

For a child left alone, the house felt enormous—full of strange creaks, shadows, and the scurrying of rats sometimes in the basement. I was often convinced someone was looking in through the windows.

Rock music and reading became my solace, quieting the noise inside and outside my head long enough for me to fall asleep.

And, then...

Boom! And there it was. The unmistakable sound of the leaded glass front door being slammed shut. The sound I'd been dreading. It woke me from my sleep, signaling: *The bar is here! After party at the Somervilles.*

Loud music, laughter and voices reverberated throughout the house. The smell of marijuana wafted up to my room and drunk partygoers lined up in the hallway outside my door waiting for the bathroom.

I would put a pillow over my head trying to drown out the noise because in just a few hours, I would need to put on my uniform, grab a cold piece of Sonny's pizza for breakfast, and make my way to school where people like Sister Leo were waiting to squash my dreams.

Often, I would fall asleep in class, and a note would accompany me home. Someone would notice it tacked to the refrigerator and eventually it would get signed. If it wasn't my mother's signature, it didn't matter. Everyone in the OLA parish knew the tragedy our family endured, and we were doing the best we could.

As the siblings moved out and away, their rooms were quickly filled family friends who needed a place to live but couldn't quite afford market rent. We took them in because after all the mortgage still needed to be paid, and no one was going to force my mother out of the house. My grandparents made that perfectly clear in their will. That home could not be sold until everyone was settled. At least that was the tale she told me.

A new tenant meant a new bedroom for me. I was constantly being relocated and displaced within my own home. At one point I had the whole 3rd floor dormitory to myself, another time I shared it with a few young women. However, once I was forced to double-up with my mother, the front cut-through bedroom, was firmly mine. I interfered with her love life and quest to find a man.

With less actual Somervilles living in the house the more depraved the conditions became and the less tolerant I would become. Pre-teen Sharon would often stomp down the stairs, march to the volume button on the built-in hi-fi, turn the music down and yell, "There is a *child* sleeping upstairs who needs to get up in a few hours for school!!"

At that point, I was usually reminded that I was a child and shouldn't talk to adults like that and the music would reach the level it was by the time I made it back to my bedroom. *What was it that Winston Churchill used to say?* I'd muttered to myself on my way up. The answer came as I'm covering my ears with the pillow, "Children should be seen not heard."

Sigh. And so it goes.

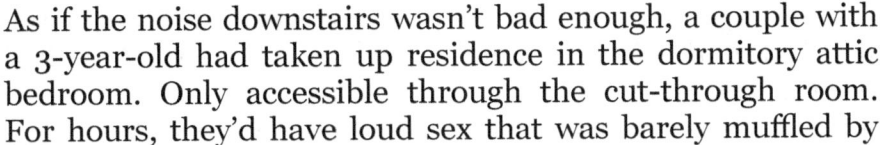

As if the noise downstairs wasn't bad enough, a couple with a 3-year-old had taken up residence in the dormitory attic bedroom. Only accessible through the cut-through room. For hours, they'd have loud sex that was barely muffled by the closed door between the cut-through room. No regard for anyone else in the house.

Eventually, I snapped. Opened the door and I yelled up the stairs, "Please, for the love of God, stop! If not for me, for your kid! She's like three feet away from you!" and I slammed the door shut.

It fell on deaf ears. That old cut-through bedroom—once a childhood luxury—had become my own personal hell.

Life became survival mode while I clung to the memories of better days and devised a plan to escape. I'd put on a brave face and, when needed, grab Robin and retreat into the closet floor for a good cry, curling up in a ball, making myself as small as I felt.

And, just when I thought things couldn't possibly get worse, at the age of thirteen, my 35-year-old mother married my brother Marty's 18-year-old best friend, Kenny.

Let me say that again. When I was thirteen years old, my 35-year-old mother married my brother Marty's 18-year-old best friend, Kenny.

Kenny was a raging alcoholic with a cocaine problem who, later, without Marty always around, had a penchant for bringing home unsavory friends—men with lecherous stares. Shortly following their marriage, we moved out of the Somerville family home so my mother could live out her 1950s housewife fantasy. She actually quit her job! A fantasy indeed! That doesn't even qualify for a spot in the princess genre.

The whole nightmare finally ended with taking his own life a few weeks following my high-school graduation, nearly taking ours on his way out.

The only good thing about the Kenny years, was my mom briefly found sobriety about two years in. Now I only had to deal with his violent outbursts, not hers. And I owed this joker no loyalty. I'd survived this long without a father, and I certainly wasn't going to let a coke head alcoholic tell me what to do.

And, when he beat the shit out of her, ripped our house apart, held a gun to her head and/or tried to come into my room at night, I simply picked up the phone and Marty was over in a hot minute to take me out of the situation and take me home. Marty and his wife had bought our family home on Allien after we moved out. I spent long stretches at their house making myself useful by watching my three rambunctious nephews.

My mother would make me come back home, sometimes out of principal (*Sharon, I am your mother!*), guilt (*Honey, I am your mother*) or the promise things would be different. Kenny was going to rehab, again. Oh joy!

Make no mistake—I loved my mother and have plenty of joyful memories of her. But the scars she left ran deep. The older I got, the more I found myself both admiring her and aching for her. Two things can be true. Champagne does pair quite nicely with hashbrowns.

She carried more than her share: the fourth oldest, a single mother with no support from my father, and a daughter who lost both her parents back-to-back in her early thirties. She was pretty. She was talented. She was an artist. A small business owner. A homeowner. And honestly, in many ways, she was just doing what most twenty- or thirty-somethings do—going out with friends, chasing love, or at least a good time. Having a bar in the family and a big house for the after-party didn't hurt her popularity.

What she didn't do was protect me or make me a priority. She never made me feel safe or like I was the most important person in her world. Instead, I often became the reason for her frustration—the scapegoat for everything that went wrong. More than once, she called me an ungrateful little bitch, reminding me how lucky I was not to have grown up in an orphanage. It was emotional neglect wrapped in martyrdom— the classic pattern of the emotionally unavailable parent.

And boy, I absorbed that generational trauma like the sponge I am. I stuffed it way down there and learned to live with it. It was not only my badge of honor, but it was what was holding me back. Adult children of emotionally immature parents often feel frustrated, angry, rejected, and lonely. After all, how can we move past the trauma of our formative years and lead fulfilled lives if we're still burdened by the issues of our caregivers? (*a truth I would only later have language for*)

I wouldn't fully figure this out for a long time.

For a smart girl like me, it was soul-crushing to finally realize this. It was literally right there. It was the rusted sign I ignored throughout my life as I was driving toward my shiny life.

Chapter 7:
Not for You

FRESH OFF THE heels of Kenny's suicide, I took up residency in an all-girls dormitory called Marycrest at the University of Dayton. It wasn't an Ivy, but I did it! I made it! I survived my childhood, and now here I was at a catholic school that offered the comfort and safety that comes from familiarity.

Living in an all-girls dormitory harkened back to the days of my all-girls high school. While there weren't a whole lot of students from my alma mater, St. Joseph Academy (for girls), there were plenty of Cleveland West-siders from West Park and the neighboring suburbs of Bay Village, Rocky River, and Avon Lake. And, since many of the girls came from SJA's rival school, Rocky River's Magnificat, we could find common ground—first as frenemies and then as allies. After four years of same-sex Catholic schooling, we weren't seeking sorority life.

Been there, done that.

We came from a strong sisterhood. My ride or dies affectionately refer to each other as the West Park Coven (Heather, Margaret, Lisa, and sometimes Barb). Salem 1692, you missed more than one. Typical of an overachiever, we peaked early.

It was thanks to my high school guidance counselors who recognized that my smarts could translate into scholarships and thanks to a family discount via my uncle Jack, a Marianist Brother, the University of Dayton (UD) was affordable.

UD was founded by and run by the Marianist order. Jack

worked on the campus (as a pipefitter, of course) and lived just a short walk away from my dorm room. This provided convenience for my family, as the Marianist community house had plenty of space to put up our convoy for the weekend and future visits.

It only took four Somervilles, five if you count Jack, to drop me off at the University of Dayton (Mom, Ruthie, Marty, and Karen). But what came before that was nothing short of a victory lap. This celebratory excursion was preceded by a full family-and-friends weekend at Apple Valley, a resort-style planned community we had access to thanks to Kenny's parents—Ohio's version of the Catskills.

That weekend was loud, proud, and joyful. The kind of gathering that proves it takes a village—and that my village is a fucking blast.

But I remember thinking that weekend, *you mean people have second homes? You just leave stuff here? You can drive down anytime and vacation?*

I had no idea this kind of life existed outside of movies and glossy magazines and was in the reach of "normal" people. But I knew immediately that 'resort life' was for me, and it was officially added to the bucket list.

While most freshmen enter college undecided, I knew exactly who I was going to be. I proudly registered on my first day as an English Major and a pre-law student. After all, I'd spent my whole life preparing to win arguments and feel heard.

When people asked what I wanted to be, it was simple: doctor or lawyer. And since blood and I have never been on speaking terms, lawyer it was. (Although I didn't take a PhD off the table –titles have always appealed to me).

Law had everything I loved—drama, strategy, storytelling, and the sweet satisfaction of being right. I was determined, confident, and certain that the world was about to meet its next Supreme Court Justice or Madame President. Oh, and

I of course, wanted to be a writer. What do lawyers do? They research, write and argue. Perfect.

Okay, full disclosure—I spent most of high school majoring in partying and minoring in questionable decisions. My friend group was the blueprint for every '80s high school movie: *Valley Girl, Sixteen Candles,* and—slightly outside the era—*Can't Hardly Wait.* We were also very much like the group from *The Big Chill*—minus their devotion to Xichigan football.

Had I applied myself, I probably could have gotten into an Ivy. Regretful? Sure. But would I trade the experiences I had and the lifelong memories I made with friends who are still in my life today? No way.

Still, something shifted when I got to Dayton. Two months in, I looked around and realized a party girl doesn't become a lawyer or Madame President – we had much higher standards back then. Gary Hart had to drop out of the presidential race for an affair and John Kerry was vilified for his treatment of his wife, Teresa Heinz Kerry, dying of breast cancer. Bill Clinton didn't inhale that marijuana cigarette and Jimmy Carter read *PLAYBOY* — clutch those pearls. *Yet, somehow, in 2024, a convicted felon sits in the Oval Office. (SMDH)*

One drunken night in my friend Katie's dorm room, I caught my reflection in the mirror and didn't like who I saw. So, I quit. Cold turkey. Didn't touch a drop again until my last college final four and a half years later—and that night, well, that's another story.

What this reformed party girl did become was unexpectedly pregnant by the end of my freshman year. That was certainly not in the plan. Ahh. The best laid plans of *Mice and Men.*

After telling the father, my next call was to Marty. *C*RAP!

Fortunately, this happened near the end of the semester, and I'd be home in a week.

Marty's reaction... "Don't worry, Sha. We'll figure this out together." Always looking out for his sister.

So, I came home and Marty lived up to his promise...we'll figure this out together...I went to Marty's the minute I got home from Dayton. *Crap...what the hell were we going to do? But he promised that he had the answer and that he would help me.*

I was so nervous on the drive over there. *How could I screw up like this? How could I have been so stupid? A smart, ambitious girl like me didn't let something like this happen. I ruined everything! How was I going to tell everyone? What would they think of me? What the hell was I going to do?*

Marty would know what to do. I trusted him. He loved me unconditionally and never judged me. After all, the same thing had happened to him—and a few others in our family. I just worried he'd give me the obvious answer: shotgun wedding, have the baby, get a job, keep moving. That plan had worked for plenty of people in our family. But I was different, and deep down, I knew that wasn't the right path for me. Everyone had their own hopes and expectations for my life—and I had mine, too.

By the end of my freshman year at Dayton, I was emaciated. My anxiety was at an all-time high. With alcohol no longer dulling the senses, I experienced crippling panic attacks. I stopped going to class, eating and barely left my room. Quickly, I became convinced that there was something really wrong with me and that I was going to die. On my first visit to student health services, they told me my blood sugar was low. I needed to eat better. On my second visit to student health services, they told me I was suffering from exhaustion. I needed to sleep and drink more water. On my third visit to the student health center, they told me I was pregnant.

I finally arrived at Marty's and my childhood home. Safe.

He was waiting on the porch, and as I approach the steps he said, "are you sure you're pregnant? You look like shit! *(thanks Bro. love you too)* When was the last time you ate?"

I said "months" and then with tearing streaming down my

face; he swallowed my skeletal frame into his teddy bear body and all I could say was "I'm so sorry. I totally fucked-up!"

He let go and said, "well what are you going to do?"

I stood there; I didn't expect a question! I expected an answer or at the very least advice. I waited. Nothing.

So, finally I broke the stare and silence and said, "For the first time in my life, I have NO idea."

"Well, what do you want to do?" he said.

Again, I said, "For the first time in my life, I have NO idea."

I'm pretty sure I added, "I have no fucking idea."

We went inside, and much to my surprise, he didn't have the answers. We talked for hours—about my beliefs, my thoughts, my fears, my dreams. He questioned everything. Were my beliefs really mine? After all, I'd been raised a good Catholic girl, taught that abortion was the evilest word in the English language. He asked about my ambitions, my vision for the future. Was I absolutely sure a baby couldn't fit into it? He wanted to know who else in the family knew. Of course, he was the only one I'd told.

By the end of the day, we still didn't have answers or a plan. He stood firm—it was my decision, not his. Which was ironic, because that was exactly why I'd gone to him. What we did have was an understanding—that we'd figure it out together, and that he'd love me and support me no matter what.

Over the next few weeks, my thoughts went back and forth. We all know what those options are, so I won't elaborate. Unlike my mother, I *had* a choice. (RIP **Roe v. Wade** 1973-2022)

One night, I thought I'd finally made my decision. It was late, but never too late to call Marty.

"I've decided," I told him. "I'll be over first thing in the morning."

When I arrived, I did all the talking. I was resolute and

determined—in a way that only I could be. I told him I'd decided to give the baby up for adoption. It was the best option. I wasn't ready to be a mom, I wasn't ready to be a wife to someone I wasn't sure I wanted to marry, and I knew I couldn't terminate the pregnancy. That wasn't Catholic guilt talking—it was just my truth. Adoption felt like the only path I could live with. I'd carry the baby, hope for a good family, and somehow move on with my life.

Marty sat quietly for what felt like forever before saying, "After you called last night, I kinda knew this is what you'd decide. So, I talked to my wife, and we decided we can't let that happen. This baby is a Somerville—our family, our blood. We've already lost too much to let this one go to strangers. But if that's what you really want, then Diane and I are going to adopt the baby."

To this day, I don't know if he'd actually talked to his wife or if it was just his gut reaction. I could have asked her—but that wasn't the point. What mattered was the gesture. He meant it. He was ready to step in without hesitation. And while I didn't take him up on his offer, that moment gave me exactly what I needed: the courage—and the safety net—to keep going.

I moved home to Cleveland, transferred to John Carroll University and married (in that order). It was just a bump in the road, but I was still on the right course. I went to school until I was 9 months pregnant, took the winter semester off to have my baby and returned that fall to finish my degree and graduate top of my class. There's a picture of me in my cap and gown, holding my 3-year-old daughter in one arm and my BA in the other. I thought the hard part was over. Turns out, it was just beginning.

As I approached graduation with hopes still to go to law school, I was invited to pursue the opportunity to earn my master's degree in English as a graduate teaching assistant. Free tuition and a stipend to boot! After years of scraping by, it was a no-brainer. Plus, I thought having a teaching assistantship and a master's degree would only increase my chances at a scholarship to law school. Still on the right path. Nothing can stop me now.

Instead, here is what happened. I finished grad school, which turned out to be the best two years of my life. I had my first real taste of validation and stability. Those two years were oxygen. Teaching, reading, and writing became a safe haven of intellect and purpose. Plus, I had a gift for understanding, interpreting, and explaining William Shakespeare of all people. The girl who once skimmed the cliff notes of *Hamlet* was now presenting her theories about the absent mother motif to a group of PhDs at a conference held at the University of Florida. And I was still only a graduate student! I was quickly making my mark as an up-and-coming Shakespearean Scholar. A very niche and prestigious sect within academia. I mean, how many Shakespearean Scholars do you know?

So long, lawyer. Hello, Doctor Somerville.

But oxygen only lasts as long as the tank. Eventually, reality taps you on the shoulder. The demands of motherhood, a failing marriage, and the desire to make a home for my daughter (i.e., buying a home) put my dreams on hold. Once again, I pivoted. Only this time, I wasn't saving myself; I was saving stability for her. So, instead of pursuing a law degree or a PhD, I chose to begin working. At the time, I thought, okay another bump in the road. I'm young, I'll be 38 when Meg goes off to college. There is still plenty of time.

Flash forward. I'm now in my early 50s, and I'm still waiting. Anxious, restless, self-doubting, self-deprecating, depressed, and in my mind, running out of time. Waiting turned into a habit fueled by procrastination, untreated trauma, and a lifetime of grief. It provided the proof that I made all the wrong choices.

I mean what does one *do* with a degree in Shakespearean literature? When was the last time you saw a job posting for *Wanted: Shakespearean Scholar*... I'll wait.

Now from the outside, I have a fabulous, shiny life with a

laundry list of cool experiences. My sheer grit and determination parlayed into a career in event planning and nonprofit work. Turns out all that partying in high school actually paid off! I'm considered a leader in my field and am known for turning a champagne toast into a fundraising strategy.

I've been part of the planning for some of Cleveland's most notorious celebrations—the opening of the Rock and Roll Hall of Fame, the NBA's 50th Anniversary (Snoop Dogg performed), two World Series parties (we lost both), and the city's bicentennial. I've partied on the roof of the Rock Hall with Tina Turner's band during her private Christmas party, sat stage-side with my 8-year-old daughter at a Mandy Moore concert, and made her dream come true when we went backstage for photos, and have an autographed Stephen King book from an intimate Sarasota reading of *Sleeping Beauties*. I've also raised millions for the charities I love—the work that actually changes the world and not just the guest list.

My second marriage was on a beach in Jamaica. I traveled to Amsterdam to see Pearl Jam for my fiftieth birthday. Quite the life—shiny, fabulous, and full of champagne and hashbrowns

Yet still, I wonder—all the time—what if? What if I'd kept going? What if I'd believed I deserved to?

Non-profit fundraising isn't the most stable career. In the mid- 90s there were no degrees or certificates in non-profit management. The CFRE credential (Certified Fundraising Executive), which emerged in the early 1990s, was expensive, rare, and required several CE credits and experience. None of which I had the time or money for. I wouldn't earn mine until 2022. I was in constant fear that it could all disappear in a moment. Then what?

Armed with the skills of organization, storytelling, people-reading, and survival, I forged ahead. Problem-solving became my superpower, and I always delivered the results. What I traded in salary was access to cool experiences, flexibility to raise my family, and dealing with Marc's unpredictable health

(MS likes to rear its ugly head at the worst time). Plus, if I had to be away from my children, I at least wanted that time to be used for good, something towards making the world a better place. I wanted them to have a mom that they could be proud of, depend on, and who always put their needs first. In other words, I wanted them to have the safety, stability, and the mother I never had.

And, for the most part, I did. But beneath the busy, competent surface, a whisper remained. A line I couldn't shake from *Little Women*, when Jo says, "I should have been a great many things."

That's me. I should have been a great many things. But maybe, just maybe the truth is – I already am.

Chapter 8:
Passionately Exhausted

SINCE I ESSENTIALLY learned nothing in college that applied to the actual mechanics of corporate life, every job I ever walked into was a blank slate. There were "rules" sure— but nothing absolute. X didn't always equal Y. The auditors might have been balancing books; I was busy trying to balance my life—and trying to figure out who I was going to be when I grew up, now that being a lawyer or a doctor was off the table.

I landed at the Cleveland Chamber of Commerce, at the time, the largest Chamber of Commerce in the country, with 16,000 members. There I began making a study of the women around me—how they dressed, how they carried themselves, how they managed to sound confident even when you could see the uncertainty flicker behind their eyes. I didn't realize it then, but I was collecting data. Field research on how to survive in a world that rewards perfection and punishes pause. Where a smart suit, pantyhose, and being part of the 5 a.m. club were required to get ahead.

At the Chamber, I had access to all kinds of cool things— events, connections, glimpses of power. In fact, I was even asked to plan our CEO's retirement party, where the guest of honor was none other than Coretta Scott King. I was not only in charge of Ms. Hoover's party, but also of all of Mrs. King's travel arrangements. Me, the girl with the English degree.

But access has a way of stirring up envy, and the green-eyed monster was never far from my side. I watched women business owners' stride into meetings with confidence I could only mimic. Comparison became my full-time side hustle.

So, I did what any overachieving perfectionist would do—I took advantage of the business planning course we were charging Chamber members thousands of dollars to attend. I never turn down a free opportunity to learn. It confirmed what I already suspected: I had the entrepreneurial mind, but not the entrepreneurial courage. Failure wasn't an option; it was a threat. I was a mom with a house payment.

So instead of leaping, I kept climbing—planning events for a living while my personal life spun in chaos wrapped in sparkles. I mean, I do love anything that sparkles.

There were mentors, sure—the kind who'd say, "Come to the mixer, make the connections, stay visible." But I was already working too much. The idea of "after hours" or giving more felt laughable. I was chasing the 40 Under 40 list, attending Rock Hall events, concerts, galas—living what looked like a cool life.

And maybe it was. From the outside.

Inside, I was just trying to stay upright, keeping the image polished while quietly falling apart underneath it all. I was part of the 5 AM club, but my membership looked a little different. After my first marriage failed, I quickly jumped into my second. Although we dated for 12 years before we married, Marc was indeed my person.

He came with more baggage than I did, if only because he was 11 years ahead of me. I came with a house and an 8-year-old, and a reckless abandonment that would be fueled by the loss of my brother. Dying young in my family appeared to be the Somerville curse. I'd better get a move on.

Marc came with three kids, two former wives, alimony, and child support payments. He worked two jobs to make ends meet. And, when we finally did marry, I didn't mind being his third because after all, three is a magic number!

He also came with a debilitating illness, MS, later complicated by a seizure disorder. I didn't know that right away, however. At the time, Marc showed no signs.

The first time we went "out" wasn't dinner or a movie. It was a tattoo parlor in Euclid. I was 28, ink-free, terrified of needles; Marc was 39 and had about fourteen tattoos already—and was apparently getting his "last one." *Spoiler alert: it wasn't.*

I walked in clutching a Disney VHS of *Peter Pan*. The artist looked at me like, *what in the hell is this?* But I knew exactly what I wanted. And Marc. Well, he looked at me like, with his devilish grin, thinking, *who is this girl?* The way you look at the next "it girl" or if you saw a unicorn.

For me, tattoos had to mean something. And I knew this would—because what I was choosing wasn't just an image, it was a piece of my story.

Shortly after we moved back into Allien, after my grandparents died—when I took up residency in the attic dormitory with Ruthie, Annie, and Peggy—I had a dream I've never forgotten.

I was lost in Disneyland, running down Main Street, crying for my mom. Although I had never been to either Disney Park, we watched the Wonderful World of Disney every Sunday night, so I knew exactly what it looked like.

Then I saw my grandparents—calm, familiar, safe. I ran up and hugged them, so relieved. My grandmother, who always promised to take me to ride the carousel at Disney, looked at me and said, "She's with us. You must go now. You're not meant to be here."

Then they turned and walked toward Sleepy Beauty's Castle, where the carousel lay in wait on the other side of the castle.

I knew what that meant—she was dead. Weirdly, I wasn't afraid. Disney was not only the happiest place on earth. It was the safest. Nothing bad happens at Disney. I already understood that life moves forward, with or without your permission. I got this.

So, when I thought about that first tattoo, I chose Tinkerbell. Faith. Hope. Pixie Dust. The three things I've leaned on my entire life, even when everything else felt heavy.

Not long after, Marty was in a car accident that would ultimately claim his life after fourteen long days. My tattoo was still healing, and now my heart carried a matching open wound. Without Marty, I was all alone on this Boulevard of Broken Dreams. Depression crept in, anxiety took over, and avoidance became my only coping mechanism. The signs I kept seeing around me started to feel less like coincidences and more like self-fulfilling prophecies.

For example, Marc called me up one day and invited me to lunch so we could "talk." I knew what that meant. *Well, that was fun while it lasted.* And at least I have a good story about this tattoo. I tried to tell myself when I was totally bummed. I thought this was different. Guess I missed the signs. To mask my heartache, I would assume my power position – the upper hand.

I marched into the restaurant, sat down, and said, "I know why I'm here. You don't have to say it. I'm not going to sit here and make small talk while we enjoy our last meal together and agree to part 'friends.'"

Marc grabbed my arm as I started to leave, and said, "Sit down, you don't know a thing."

"What did he just say?" Nothing stops me dead in my tracks faster than being told I'm wrong.

Marc took a breath. "I just feel like we've reached the point where you should know—I have MS."

All I could do was laugh. *Nice one, universe.*

"Isn't this rich?" I said as I sat back down and lit a cigarette. "You've got to be fucking kidding me. That's it? That's what I've been afraid of?"

Same feeling I had the first time I talked to my father—years of buildup, stomach in knots, then the big reveal lands with a thud. *Fun fact: the castle at Disneyland, big disappointment, too.* Not Disney World, Disneyland.

"That's it? That's what you needed to talk about? Don't ever call a girl and say, *'we need to talk'* unless you're breaking up with her."

"Well, how should I have said it?" he questioned.

"I don't know—but not like that."

"Did you even hear what I said? I have MS. Do you even know what that is?" he asked again.

"All too well, honey. My mom has MS." I didn't say it like a confession. Just a fact.

Jesus, I'll never shake my childhood. But I'm sure going to try. I'll show her I'm not the problem. You can live a great life with MS. I'm not her.

Just as I predicted, because I was giving all my time, energy, and money to my new life. My relationship with my mother suffered. That, and she started drinking again. While I put up with her shit when I didn't have a choice, now that I was a mom, there were boundaries. There was no way I was going to let my daughter relive my childhood. No way in hell.

What followed was a vicious cycle—jealousy, distance, guilt. Eventually, *she* cut it off. It was never enough. I was never enough.

See, even your mom doesn't love you. In fact, Sharon, neither of your parents loves you.

That voice—the one that's lived rent-free in my head for decades—fed both my hunger to succeed (*I'll show them!*) and my anxiety (*You're going to fail!*) until it was gluttonously full. It disguised itself as ambition: Type-A, highly organized, exceptional work ethic, always performing. But it also morphed into anger, irritability, that short fuse that came out when my plate was so overloaded, things started falling off the edge—and the dog was eating it.

People either marveled—"I don't know how you do it all!"—or whispered, "OMG, she's such a bitch," when things weren't going according to plan. A supervisor once wrote in my annual review:

> "Sharon is the person you always want in your foxhole when you're going to battle. She's tenacious, fiercely loyal, and will work long and hard to get the job done. However, she's somewhat of a loose cannon. The problem is you just don't know which Sharon is going to show up on any given day."

For years, I shrugged it off, but not before replaying that criticism repeatedly. I would conclude:

That's just my personality. Take it or leave it.

I'm direct. I've got a lot going on. If you only knew the day I've had.

Geez, relax—you know I'll get the job done.

But the thing that really burned me? Watching my male counterparts get away with so much more. Their "assertiveness" was leadership. Their outbursts were "passion."

Their mistakes were "learning opportunities." Meanwhile, I was too much. Too direct. Too emotional. Too loud. Too something.

Since I never really had mentors or role models to look up to, I made it up as I went—fueled by equal parts ambition and survival. So, when I was called out for my tone or sharp edges, it didn't just sting; it confirmed the story I'd been told my whole life. *See, you really aren't enough. You're flawed. You're unworthy. You'll never be her. You're a fraud.*

At the chamber, I was usually the event planner, so I rarely got to attend business events as a guest. But one day, I was invited to a Women in Business luncheon hosted by a local business journal that was one of our members. I was at a particularly low point—overwhelmed, restless, stretched so thin between who I was and who I was trying to be.

I'd just been promoted to Director, which sounded great on paper, but the trade-off for the title and the slightly higher salary was... more work. I didn't negotiate, didn't advocate for a fair wage—just took what was offered. Later, I found out by accident that I was making significantly less than other directors. Classic. For the girl with expensive taste, I didn't see the value I held. I was damaged goods. So of course, I was on the sale rack.

Still, I thought, *maybe this luncheon will be different.* A room full of women who'd understand. Women lifting women—the kind of energy you get at International Women's Day events now. If I hadn't told myself that, I probably would've spent the whole week coming up with creative excuses to back out while still sounding "grateful." Truth was, I didn't think I had it in me.

It was a three-person panel: A woman in banking—a trailblazer. A woman in construction—a trailblazer. And a woman who was the first female President and CEO of one of the largest national retailers headquartered in Northeast Ohio. Everyone knew that brand. Everyone leaned in, hanging on every word, imagining themselves up there someday—me included.

Then came the Q&A. I stood up, a young professional, divorced mom with small kids, trying desperately to make it all work, and asked: "How do you balance it all without losing your mind?" This was before "self-care" was a thing. Before we talked about burnout, mental health, or boundaries. The answers rolled in:

> "Well, I don't sleep. I'm at the gym every morning by 4:30 AM. I get all my alone time before anyone wakes, and I head into the office."

"I couple my love of reading with books that sharpen the saw. I highly recommend *The 7 Habits of Highly Effective People*."

Yeah, I'd tried that—I had the planner, color-coded and covered in stickers like a teenager's diary. But I never really followed the plan. My stickers were a great conversation starter, though. That, and the fact that I signed off all my emails with "Have a Magical Day"

Then the CEO spoke. She said, "Well, I made the decision years ago never to have children. My mother and father were both executives, and I never saw them. I didn't want to do that to my children."

Wait—what? Did she just say you can't do both? That it is selfish to even try?

That was her advice to a room full of women.

I was crushed. It was already over before I'd even started.

That day, I didn't walk out feeling inspired—I walked out feeling small. Defeated. Passionately exhausted.

Chapter 9:
Given to Fly

I'M GOING TO be real here. I could tell you every detail about what came next, but I've traded severance for silence more than once. Quick summary, I spent a better half of my career in my hometown, Cleveland, then blew it all up in my 40s to move to Florida. I've had career highs that made me feel unstoppable, like becoming an Executive Director for a truly innovative and lifesaving national healthcare organization at the ripe old age of 32. I've had lows, too, that brought me to my knees. I've been fired more than once. Sometimes gently, sometimes with all the grace of a wrecking ball. Each time, it added fuel to the shame fire already burning in my head. *Failed again! Not worthy!* I'd spiral, question my worth, and chase the next bright, shiny thing. Reinvention, isolation, and self-destruction became my favorite coping mechanisms.

I own my part in it. I over functioned, glorified my work ethic, clung to my high standard of excellence, lost my temper, and built walls instead of bridges. I flew too close to the sun with wax wings. I was the mean girl. I didn't ask for help.

I tried to save the world and everyone in it, alone, because that's what trauma-trained people do, and it's all I've known. I was always on high alert. Ready for battle. I've also been passionate about every cause I've ever worked for. I give it everything I've got, every time. And boy, you'll find no one more loyal than me. I mean, hello—die-hard Browns fan. That should tell you everything you need to know about sticking it out when the odds are terrible, and the payoff almost never comes. *Still waiting for next year.*

That's the culture of nonprofit work, though. You're expected to accept less—less pay, less benefits, less stability—and call it "purpose." You're told it's noble to be exhausted, admirable to sacrifice your own well-being for the greater good. I believe it's called "compassion fatigue." Which sounds fine, until you realize how perfectly it feeds the self-doubt of people who already question their worth. After 20+ years in this profession, no wonder I thought about driving off a damn bridge.

The nonprofit world is full of light, but there's a dark underside no one likes to talk about. Power imbalances dressed up as "mission." The hero complex is rewarded, and burnout romanticized. Don't even get me started on rogue boards or rubber-stamp boards. I'm not sure which is the lesser of two evils. It's why fundraisers either last twelve months or twelve years. The quick hit isn't just about finding the next pay increase; it's often about escaping toxicity packaged as "team culture."

The pandemic cracked the illusion. Mental health became the word of the day. Every organization had its "we care about you" campaign or "kumbaya moments via Zoom." *Fun Fact: cake and pizza parties don't heal trauma.* And I'm not talking just about my own personal PSTD here. The pandemic was legit a traumatic event. Just like hurricanes, school shootings, or women losing agency over their bodies. Casual Fridays don't fix a toxic environment or erase systemic dysfunction. And therapy stipends, chair messages, or EAPs mean nothing if your culture still rewards (or demands) martyrdom. Unlimited vacation sounds good on paper but try getting your PTO approved. Sure, these "perks" are all nice. Progress over perfection, right? But real change requires real truth, and most workplaces still can't handle that conversation.

If any employers out there are truly listening, please do. If your employees are burned out and turnover is high, take a good look in the mirror and don't just put a band-aid on a gunshot wound. When you're looking for budget cuts, hands off professional development, raises, and bonuses, support your people. Did none of you see *National Lampoon's Christmas Vacation?*

I can't tell every story here—some are mine, many were entrusted to me—and I won't name names. But patterns don't need attribution to be true. Nothing here is about a single organization. It's about what gets normalized when power goes unchecked.

I'm certainly no HR expert, but after decades in the workforce, here's a short list of what not to do:

1. Don't fire someone by text or email and call it "a sign of the times." Don't fly them to your corporate headquarters, fire them, and then put them back on a plane, all in the name of "the courtesy of telling you in person." Video conferencing exists, as does the telephone. You probably have one within arm's reach right now. Kindness matters.

2. Don't hide behind a "Performance Improvement Plan" when the outcome has already been decided. Don't dress an exit strategy up as employee development and then fire someone when they predictably "fail." And for heaven's sake, don't do it on a Monday at the end of the day. Aren't Mondays bad enough? Extra points for not doing it the night before the holiday party their team planned. Timing is leadership. Use it better.

3. Don't blindside your head fundraiser about "leadership changes" the morning right before surgery, during a critical campaign moment, or while they're thousands of miles from home.

4. Don't encourage a woman to step forward for the top job, let her do the emotional labor of believing you, and then quietly hand it to someone with no nonprofit leadership experience. If you're not serious, don't ask. And don't be shocked when people stop trusting the process.

5. Don't prioritize a donor, board member, or "star" client over your staff—especially when that person is harassing them, famous, or both. **Don't negotiate with people who use power or money as leverage.** No gift is worth your integrity. Choosing to protect people over power is what being an Upstander actually looks like. Culture always tells the truth.

Workplaces love to talk about "family," until it's inconvenient. Loyalty is a one-way street. And those of us who kept showing up—out of fear, duty, or some broken idea of resilience—pay a very high price, in anxiety, health, and self-respect.

My therapist once looked me dead in the eye and asked, "When will you stop abusing yourself? Why do you say no more for others but not to yourself? When will you truly break this cycle, you're so desperate to break.?"

It stopped me cold. Because I knew the answer wasn't about work, or being a caretaker, or a perfectionist—it was about me. *See I told you!* But just like every word, phrase, metaphor, analogy, there are many ways to interpret it. Words rarely mean just one thing. They bend and expand to fit the story we need them to tell.

I had to stop abusing myself in the name of being "a team player." Stop confusing trauma bonding with team building. Stop performing stability for people who would replace me without hesitation. Stop giving myself away to people who only take advantage of it—personally and professionally.

So, I stopped. Cold turkey. Just like when I quit smoking, which, if you've ever smoked or overcome any addiction, you know how difficult that is. Talk about a mind-fuck. Even 15+ years later, I face temptation. Lured by the devil on my shoulder, saying, "Just one won't kill you." Some occasions are harder than others.

I rebuilt. This time, on my terms—with boundaries, with humor, with the audacity to rest. Call me a snowflake, woke, crazy, difficult, hell, call me a heartless bitch - whatever helps you sleep at night.

I've rewritten the word *survival* into clarity.

Part 3:
Pulling Robin Out of the Suitcase

Chapter 10:
Daughter

MY CHILDHOOD WAS buried with my grandparents.

My fear faded with Kenny.

My safety vanished with Marty.

My north star dimmed with Ruthie.

My hope died with my mother.

When my mother died in 2020, it wasn't grief that hit me first. It was the familiarity of it—that sharp, sudden absence I'd known my whole life. No good-bye. No terms of endearment moment. No warning.

I simply got a phone call from Ray saying "Sha, I have some bad news. Your mother died."

Stunned.

I didn't ask how or where. I just said, "Okay," and then paused a minute before I continued, "Have you decided what you guys are going to do?"

He let me know she wanted to be cremated, no wake, mass at OLA on Saturday.

So, plans have already been made, I thought, okay then. I wonder if I'll even be in the obituary. I've been left out before.

"Well, I need a minute to process this. Not sure who else in the family knows yet, but please let me call Meggie. I don't want her it from anyone but me. And, then I'll decide if I'm going to come up to Cleveland or not. I'll text you when I get done talking to Meg and let you know."

"Okay, sweetie. Just let us know," he replied and we said our good-byes and I love yous.

But before I hung up, I said, "Hey, Ray... thank you."

He knew that I meant not just for the phone call, but for all of it.

I called Meggie and shared the news. She was equally as vanilla. Like, me, she had pre-grieved and made peace with not having her grandmother in her life. Her choice, her loss was our collective attitude. We were protecting our peace at all costs. Breaking generational trauma and living our best lives. But we both agreed, that boycotting the funeral would be out of spite and that wasn't healthy. Just like when I would open my home to the family when Ruthie died, we said "Ohana."

Ohana means family and family means no one gets left behind or forgotten.

I sat in the stillness of my disbelief in the tranquility of my backyard. *Well, I guess that's it. End of story. The rest is silence.*

Just then the doorbell rang. WTF? No one even knew where our house was yet. We had a strict no visitor rule for this pandemic. Amazon?

It was my little sister, cousin Michelle, on my front steps. Ohana.

This was exactly what I needed. Someone who could under-stand the heaviness I was feeling in all its glorious complexity. She made our plans to travel to Cleveland.

"No, I'm fine, you don't need to come with me. No, Marc can't go; we can't risk his health. I'll have Meggie, the Coven, and the rest of the family. No, really, I'll be fine."

She didn't argue with me, she just did. She ran interference with the rest of the Somerville clan, who were blowing up my phone wondering what I was going to do, and to get a temperature on how I was *really* doing?

Honestly, knowing she was here with me brought them as much comfort as it did me. I had finally gotten to a point with the siblings that I had defended my position enough for them to stop asking to make the first move, be the bigger person, and give my mother another chance. Nope. I will not be emotionally blackmailed. They understood the ball was in her court, and I was done talking about it or asking about her. I not only moved on, but I also moved to the other side of the country. I was just fine. Even on the family pandemic Zoom calls that I arranged, when the conversation turned to my mother, I simply turned off my camera, put myself on mute, silenced my speakers, and grabbed myself another glass of water. Tuning back in once that TV commercial break was over.

That day, Michelle made me laugh as we recalled stories from our childhood. That small window of my life, when we were the good kind of *Party of Five* (me, her, my mom, her mom, and Jim).

We reminisced about how I was always the brains behind the operations of our capers.

Me: "Remember when I convinced you to climb on top of the refrigerator to get us cookies but didn't have a plan for how you were going to get down and left you there? Sorry, kid, that's as far as I go. You're on your own now." I said with a cheek click. Then giggled.

Michelle: "Shall we talk about the time you almost killed me with the Christmas tree? Honestly, Sha, you're lucky we still even talk." she retorted. *Touché.*

We agreed this was payback for me having to be the victim of Marty's hi-jinks. That's what bigs do to their littles. Those were the days. Silence. Sigh. *Marty. God she's probably so happy to see you.*

I rested my head on Michelle's shoulders *and started to cry. I let the sadness creep in.* I'm not a heartless bitch after all. It's perfectly natural to cry when one loses their mother. That is legit sad. Michelle did say another word. She saw me. Even when I couldn't yet.

After she left, a familiar pain hit me like a knife. The grief stab. I was used to grief, but this cut differently. It didn't just cut me, it mutilated me. The attack was vicious, brutal, and excruciating.

How horrible must I be that my own mother didn't even want to say good-bye to me on her death bed? She would rather have died alone not on speaking terms with her only daughter.

Although I wasn't holding out for that deathbed sap scene, I thought there would at least be some peace between us. There is literally nothing on this earth that would keep me from saying my final good-byes to Meg. Meg's tiny hand is the one I want to let go of when I reach for Marty's. Guess she wins.

Talk about a trigger.

This awakened every false belief I've **ever** carried about myself. I played the greatest-hits box set of my failures—every flaw, every wrong turn, every single thing I still hadn't accomplished—at full volume. This was the grungiest hard-rock moment. Raw. Heavy. I screamed until my throat burned, singing along with Eddie Vedder—*Don't call me daughter*—because nothing else could carry it.

At some point, I wrote a note to myself on a Post-it. Just a question about death metal. I stuck it where I could see it and kept going.

See, **IT IS ALL TRUE. My own mother died without speaking to me. My own father decided I was worthless even before he met me.** This was definitive proof. I am worthless, flawed, and quite frankly, a fraud. No matter how many sprinkles or sparkles you put on top of it.

I wept. Long and hard. This was beyond ugly crying; this was grotesque, monstrous, boogieman crying. Marc tried to console me, but he knew me well enough to know that I needed to work things out on my own. I took to my bed, pulled the covers over my head, let my mind run wild, and sobbed until exhaustion took over.

Next morning. Marc brought me an Irish coffee that I waved off. I had to go to work. *No Marc! Really, I do-- the lady doth protest. I'm not going to argue with you about this. My mom just fucking died, alright. On top of all of this! You, out of all people, should understand me!!*

Funny, I hadn't yet.

During the pandemic, I didn't learn to make sourdough starter, fall down a Bravo hole, repaint my house, or try out an IKEA hack. I worked. Hard. Our museum was shut down, we were furloughing staff, and our reserves didn't take us very far. With no ticket revenue or store revenue to count on, it had to come from fundraising. I dusted off my cape, grabbed my crown and magic wand, and put on my mask (literally). Help is on the way.

Survival mode, however, always comes with a side survivors' guilt. Having to furlough a single mom with small children is gut-wrenching. Ending someone's first job out of college with a pink slip, devastating. But, all for the good of the cause.

Indeed, these were some of my finest fundraising years, performance-wise. Side A: Transforming our signature gala into a virtual event that raised $550K the first year and then the encore, $700K+ in year two. Side B: Raising the funds to bring some of the most innovative Holocaust education tools to our museum. Hidden bonus track: I put together the initial team and strategy that ultimately procured the entire Eli Weisel collection on my way out the door.

Despite all these efforts, there was a constant pallor of doom with a pressure to do more. Something was rotten in the State of Denmark. I could feel it. Here we go again. *Spoiler alert: I was right.*

I didn't even tell my co-workers my mother died, just that I had a death in my family and I needed to go to Cleveland. I only told our CEO privately, letting her know that I was estranged from my mother, so I'll be back to work shortly. I told my stepchildren, grandchildren, and in-laws, you don't need to come to the funeral or even all the way out to the West Side to see me. Even Marc wasn't coming. It's fine.

I blamed the pandemic, of course. I planned to travel with my small pod, Michelle, Pat, Jim, and Meggie to minimize exposure. I didn't want to inconvenience anyone over my mother. We didn't even speak.

Truth was, I just didn't want to have to explain myself to people who had little to no chance of getting the why of it all. If I was going to survive the next few days, I needed to eliminate that track from my playlist as much as humanly possible. I was worried enough that my family didn't fully get it. While I typically don't care what the rest of the world thinks about me, I do care what my family thinks. When you aren't even accepted by your own parents, that type of rejection leaves the kind of scars that just when you think that wound is finally healed, something comes along that rips it right open again. The deeper the wound, the longer and harder the healing. That's just basic science.

Anxiety brain took over while I puzzled and puzzled, 'till my puzzler was sore. I came to the only conclusion I could. In crisis communication, you tell the truth and tell it first. I would need to give a eulogy. I took pen to paper and composed the following note on my iPhone:

> I sit here quietly. Like I have since I got the news a few mornings ago.
>
> It is not often that I'm at a loss for words. In fact, I was brought up being told "Sharon, that big mouth of yours

is going to get you in trouble someday". I like to think she said that, not to shut me up, but to teach me that every action you take has consequences.

Whether it was speaking your mind or keeping your baby without a father in 1969.

I never fully understood any of her choices. In fact, I hated her for most of them and vowed that in my life, every decision I made would be different.

Eventually, the conflict. The resentment. The struggles of everyday life. Tore us completely apart. Mine in my quest to be different, and hers in her jealousy.

And now she is gone. And I'm okay with that. I'm okay with where we were. Where we left it. And the fact that neither one of us felt the need to "pretense" and say empty words or be anyone else than who we truly are (and were 😬).

Because you see. We were more similar than we ever wanted to admit.

And we never did, nor never would, need to find the words to say, "I love you".

Rest In Peace, Mom. I Love You. 💜

Since I had no voice in her final arrangements, I felt I needed to get Ray and Karen's blessing to speak at her funeral—knowing full well that if it came down to it, I'd do whatever the hell I wanted. I'd pull the "she's my mom" card if I had to, just like they had so many times. Karma.

But I wasn't looking for a fight. I was just tired—tired of being the one who always had to use her voice as a weapon. People call it strength; I call it survival.

My head was so foggy. Maybe it was the grief. Maybe perimenopause. Maybe the pandemic. I'd read somewhere that the

WHO said anxiety and depression spiked 25% worldwide. Maybe that was it. Maybe it was just... everything.

I texted the "eulogy" to Ray and Karen and waited. *Oh, they are not going to like this. A strategy would need to be formed if there was any descent. I was a formidable foe.*

Nothing. Still nothing. Still nothing. Panic sets-in. Shit. I pushed it too far this time. I need some reassurance. Instead of taking it to AITA on Reddit, I put it in a private Facebook group I belonged to of like-minded Pearl Jam fans. My online sorority sisters. If I prompted it right, at least they could relate to the Pearl Jam of it all. They got the complexity. They understand the song, "Daughter". If I couldn't find any empathy there, I really pushed it this time. Shit.

Okay, all good. Likes and condolences rolled in quickly, but still no texts back from the family. The phone call didn't come until I was already in Cleveland the night before the funeral. By this point, I decided to keep that moment private.

I could hear the relief in Karen's voice when I answered her hello with "I know why you're calling. I'm not going to speak tomorrow.... Yes, I'm sure."

I got enough of the validation and supportive people around me that I needed to get through the funeral, the hall repast, and then the backyard Somerville repast. The <u>real </u>Irish sendoff. Where we drink, reminisce, laugh, and all pick our favorite song that reminds us of the dead—Somerville rules of order: the immediate next of kin controls the turntable.

Funeral for a Friend kicked off the first set with lots of Elton John (*Captain Fantastic—our first show when I was 7*) followed by Paul McCartney (*her favorite and played 17 Beatles songs at the Stadium show*), Billy Joel (*Glass Houses tour*), Prince (*Purple Rain tour*), Bruce Springsteen (*Born in the USA tour*), CSNY (*After an Indians game! Tickets $7. Heather's first show, ever.*), Lenny Kravitz (*Opened for the Stones. He was better*), and Culture Club (*yes, she even took* *me to see that cross-dresser in the late 80s. There was some serious pearl clutching back then).*

I played artists from the concerts she took me and this isn't even the full list. Those are all happy memories—except that time my coven left me following the Dead, Tom Petty, and Bob Dylan show in Akron (*LeBron's hometown, an hour outside of CLE).* I was their ride. There were no cell phones, no pagers, nothing. And there was no way I was leaving them behind, even if they did. Abandoned again.

Sprinkled in were the Somerville staples—"The Twist", "Twist and Shout", "Jailhouse Rock", "We Are Family", and "Wish You Were Here". "Tubthumping" topped off with one pulling the rest of the family we'd lost in. "Radar Love" for Marty, "Superstition" for Ruthie, "Squonk" for Peggy – she wasn't dead, but her health prevented her from being there, "Hot Stuff "for Annie, the "Coffee Song" for Gram, and "Crystal Ship", another one for my brother. As each song played, we'd tell our favorite stories, the ones that still make us laugh, the ones some people have never heard, through the lump in our throats, with the tears we just can't hold back, we raise our glasses with the Somerville toast. "Sláinte!"

Once this fest was over, *damn, that was a good show,* I got on a plane back home to Florida—and finally, put her in the rearview mirror.

I left the Museum, if for no other reason than the pandemic was finally over. I was exhausted—burned out in a way that even rest couldn't fix. I wasn't one of the extra 25% who developed anxiety or depression for the first time; mine had been riding shotgun for years. It was no wonder I needed help.

Somehow, I thought adding Lexapro, a new home, and a new job to my routine might pull me out of the funk I'd been drowning in. All the yoga, walking, meditation, journaling, sticker and retail therapy I was trying to get back to just weren't cutting it. What's the definition of insanity again? Doing the same thing repeatedly and expecting a different result. I needed a clean slate.

At first, the new job felt like a reset—a fresh start. The honeymoon phase came easy; I wanted to believe this time would be different. The work itself wasn't hard, at least not at first. I remember thinking, maybe I just see things differently.

Then the real challenges started to show—not because of anyone in particular, but because every system eventually reveals its cracks. Still, I did what I always do: rolled up my sleeves, spoke up, tried to help fix what I could.

Until suddenly, it was too much. Too direct. Too honest. Too much me.

And once again, it became about me. Or so the familiar story went.

This is the story I told Dr. B during our first Talksmith session after she asked me what brought me here today.

"Well, I have a history of anxiety and depression. Talked to my primary doctor about it—*see, I can ask for help*—and she put me on Lexapro. Apparently, a lot of people got on this during the pandemic. But I don't think it's working. I thought about driving off a bridge today on my way to work. And so I here I am."

I say it without taking a breath, in my signature deadpan, smart-aleck tone, followed by a giggle that evokes all kinds of reactions—from "Is she serious?" to "I can't believe she just said that out loud, so matter of fact."

Badass.

No, really—is she serious? That might be a problem.

"Oh, did I mention my mom died? It's complicated. I give her a quick summary. I thought I was okay, but I think my mom's death really fucked me up more than I thought. I mean, from the outside, I have zero complaints. I'm living an awesome life. Chasing the dreams and for the most part catching them. I live a big life. Heck, I even went to Amsterdam to see my favorite band for my 50th birthday. Yet, I'm just never happy. I can't focus. I snap at everyone. I really scared myself on that bridge. I think there is a something really wrong with me."

We continued.

That hour with Dr. B flew by in what felt like a nanosecond. Finally, noticing the time, I said "so what do you think?"

I think today's show was brought to you by the letters P-T-S-D is what I heard.

What? Was she listening to me at all? PTSD from what?

But the pain was so deep. That day, I had caught a glimpse of understanding of what Ruthie's post-it meant. I was clearly out of options.

"Well, how do we fix that?" I asked. "This is something I clearly didn't understand. Let's get to work."

Luckily, I'm a really good student.

Chapter 11:
Porch

MARC AND I were set to go on our first vacation since the whole Jamaica/Miami fiasco. I was getting back on that vacation horse. A little trauma wasn't going to stop me. I'm Batman, after all.

If I could survive that—arranging a life flight off the island, living in a hotel, pretending to be brave for our kids while juggling work calls because I couldn't afford to miss a paycheck (no FMLA for me; three-person office)—then this would be a cakewalk. I actually remember taking a work call while waiting for Marc's MRI. *WTF.*

So yeah, I told myself, I got this. My heart disagreed, thudding hard enough to prove otherwise. Still, I thought of everything. I even flew down to Florida one weekend in October to scout the place before booking our May trip. I was leaving nothing to chance.

- ✓ **Location:** Tampa Bay, Florida. American hospitals, family on hand, if anything goes awry, I won't have to do this alone. Plus, we were nearing becoming empty nesters, and if I was going to check moving to Florida off my bucket list, it was about time Marc start learned to love it.
- ✓ **Location:** Small St. Pete beachfront boutique hotel with a balcony, room service, a variety of on-site restaurants, beach bar with two pools, fire pit, seating, and beach cabanas. Perfect if Marc's mobility is poor. We'll still be able to enjoy our time there without leaving our hotel, and if he's having better days, we could enjoy the

larger sister hotel just 200 steps away. I counted them. In reviewing the rooms, I decided a 1-bedroom suite with a kitchen was perfect for our stay. I could stock it from the grocery store across the street with enough water, Gatorade, and snacks to combat any late-night cravings or missed breakfasts when Marc needed a little extra time to get moving.

✓ **Location:** Free on-site guest parking a luxury for family coming out to the beach and the daily rate for our rental car, nominal.

✓ **Fun factor:** The Cleveland Indians were playing the Tampa Bay Rays at Tropicana Field. Going to sporting events in other towns was akin to our concert travel and museum-going. During the season Sammy Sosa and Mark MacGuire were in their battle to break Roger Maris' homerun record, we traveled to games in both Chicago and Pittsburgh to say, "we were there!" It was a short drive from the hotel, and parking and entry to the facility were manageable. On my scouting mission, I identified the best entrance with the shortest distance to our seats.

✓ **Duration:** 6 days. Long enough to enjoy ourselves, but short enough that there was no risk of running out of Marc's medication or adding a "seizure-inducing dehydration" to our list of vacation souvenirs.

✓ **Ease of travel:** Direct flight to TPA (leaving not too early or late) with a monorail to the on-site rental car facility. So much nicer than in CLE, where you must walk outside to catch a shuttle bus, all while hauling your luggage. Even roller bags are a challenge for someone walking with a gentleman's walking stick. And there is no taking a rented luggage cart on a shuttle bus.

Despite all my planning, my procrastination kicks in when it comes to packing. You'll find me running around the house like the Tasmanian devil on departure day. Panic packing as time ticks away, and we NEED TO LEAVE NOW or risk missing our flight.

Of course, I have lists upon lists of all the things I need to pack, or more importantly, what we need for Marc. I will meticulously plan our daily itinerary and review it time and time again with Marc to make certain we have everything. Everything we could possibly need.

We review our OOTs together, and Marc will lay out his clothes, essential toiletries, and medicine; I will take care of everything else and the actual packing. I always underestimate the amount of time it takes me. This only adds additional stress on top of already being overwhelmed and, quite frankly, exhausted before we ever even step on a grain of sand.

When I'm in this state, the small triggers pile up, and it doesn't end well. The pre-vacation or event frenzy. My natural short-fuse and direct tone will turn terse; this will give way to snapping, delivered with a side of aggressiveness. This then dissolves into tears while resolving itself in roaring resentment. When I reach this boiling point, I'll declare: "I'M FUCKING DONE WITH THIS SHIT!" Stomp away and enter a state of silent scorn that under no circumstance will I ever break first!

Now you've done it. You've crossed the line. This anger has turned into a nuclear reaction.

I'll give myself a moment to retreat to the bathroom floor or behind a closed door, until I can pull it enough together (stop crying) and get back to the task at hand. Because it must be done, no one else is going to do. No one is going to pick up the pieces for me.

At this point, a familiar soundtrack starts quietly playing in the background. *I know that song! I can name that tune in blank notes.* I'm not sure how many it will take because it's barely audible. My indignation is drowning it out.

I mean, they should be laying roses feet. I'd like to see them have deal with everything I do! And, then do it better than anyone else to boot! After all, I have a sign in my office that says: 'If it wasn't for last-minute panic, nothing would get accomplished.' A gift from a co-worker.

I'll recall that day for a moment. *OMG, thank you. Ain't that the truth!* It's always a delight when I get the perfect thoughtful gift. Gift giving is my love language. I thrive on making someone's day. Apparently, it's a rarity when someone makes mine. Among the many monikers I've been given is "Hard to buy for!" Personally, I don't know why. I have so many interests – Disney, the Browns, the color Pink, my hobby of the week, anything that sparkles, and duh, Pearl Jam! While that may be true, apparently, I too have a particular brand of bougie, meets unique, meets fabulous that is usually pricey.

Do have high standards? Why yes! But impossible to buy for? Try again. This sign is evidence that it really is the thought that counts. I love it! So, see, come on. It's not that hard. Just listen to me and pay attention.

Something as simple as this sign makes me feel seen.

***

The day before we were to leave for Florida, my personal and professional to-do lists were a mile long. Of course, I was working. I had an Executive Committee meeting at 1 pm that day. I was hoping to get out of there shortly after the meeting. I still must gather all our stuff, do laundry, get the dogs situated with the sitter, clean out the food that will go bad in the fridge, take out the garbage, etc. AHHHH...

No sooner than I put my bags on my desk than the phone rings. It's Marc informing me that I now must go to UPS because no one was at home to sign for the new Kindle I had ordered. The one you can read with in the sun with no glare.

Are you flipping kidding me? Why didn't you answer the door? You were home!... Okay I don't have time to argue about this. Just give me the number on the "we missed you" slip so I can figure out where to go.

I had to pick it up TODAY because we were leaving tomorrow, there would be no time before we left, and it required a signature. By the time we returned, it would be too late to send it back, and I'd have to go through the whole purchase again, which I would put off, which would mean it would live on my to-do list for what might be eternity. *Damn it. I had crossed that one off my list already.*

Now I know that song! It's the one that goes. You did this to yourself Sharon. You procrastinate everything. You should have ordered it sooner. You should have sent it to work. When will you ever learn? You can't stick with anything! You suck! Ugh. You're going to be up all night packing. After all, when you get home, you're going to have to do work because you will have to. Because. Because. Because it should be a bad word, not fuck.

T-minus two hours until the Executive Committee panic is making its way through my body. The pit in my stomach, heart palpitations, and my hands shaking. Just breathe. Focus. Damn it, now my eye is twitching. I can no longer focus. Just breathe sounds as ridiculous as it did during childbirth.

The refrain gets louder and louder. *It's your own damn fault... Sharon. If you had done this task a week ago when you put it on your list, you wouldn't HAVE to do it before you left. You're never going to get all of this done.*

Enough!! Enough!! Enough!! My inner voice screams.

Okay. I'm going to get up and get another cup of coffee, set my timer for seven minutes. Then I'm going to rewrite my list, prioritize, and sequence what MUST get done, not before I leave the office, but for Florida. Worst case, they have wi-fi in Florida, and I'm bringing my laptop. *My laptop is on the list, right? I'd better check.*

Three is a magic number. I'll focus on three things. Then the next three. Then the next three. Recenter. Repeat. You got this.

But like the morning snooze button, the timer "repeat" gets hit 3x. And, before I know it, it's only 30 minutes until my meeting. *Sharon, if you had just done this task three days ago when you wrote it down...*Three is a Magic Number *gets so loud in my head that I have to begin singing this childhood song grunge style--Soft with an edge--Crescendoing into an angry Eddie style voice; or I'm losing it! It's Evolution Baby.*

> Three is a magic number
> Yes it is, it's a magic number
> Faith and hope and charity
> The heart, the brain and the body
> Give you three as a magic number......

By the time the Executive Committee starts, I welcome the distraction. I'm also even further behind. Ugly cry emoji.

In my haste to finish the task at hand, I rush out the door, notebook in hand, agenda, and pen. Coming in hot! Distracted and disheveled. They are clearly waiting for me, and I'm a few minutes late.

I sit down, take a quick breath, and smile. and say "Sorry! I'm in my pre-vacation mode. So much to do. So little time!" like a child who should be sent to the kid's table.

Ring. Ring. Ring. Our conference table is within earshot of my office. *Where's my cell phone? Shit, I left it on my desk! Who keeps calling me?*

Ring. Ring. Ring. *Now they are calling my office phone.*

Ring. Ring. Ring.

Ring. Ring. Ring.

I'm no longer paying attention to the half-attention I was already paying to this meeting—I'm laser-focused on who the hell is calling me.

Whoever it is! Chillax! See, I can't even get a moment's peace! It's probably Marc, calling about something insignificant, but it's a catastrophe in his mind. After all, I am married to Chicken Little.

Slightly annoyed, I think, *can't wait to see what fresh hell awaits me following this meeting.*

As I suspected, most of my missed calls are from Marc, but then I notice that both Marian and Karen have called. That's not good. They know I'm leaving tomorrow, crazy busy. They wouldn't call me at work unless something's wrong. As I begin listening to the voice mail messages, no details, just "call me as soon as you can." Then it hits me.

It's 2014, so my first thought is*: My mom! I swear to sweet baby cheezus if she f-up my vacation...I'm boiling.*

The phone rings again. It's Meggie. Sobbing so hard, I can barely make her out.

"Mom, Russ just called me. Aunt Ruthie's dead," she says.

What?!! Did she just say Ruthie? I must have misheard her.

"I think you are mistaken, honey. Are you sure it wasn't Gree?" *I reply.*

"No, Mom! It's Ruthie! Russ didn't really have any details except that Uncle Ray was over at her apartment and she's dead!" *she says.*

Convinced she's dead wrong, I consoled her and said, "Sit tight. Marian and Karen both called me. I highly doubt it's Ruthie. We just saw her at Rachel's wedding on Saturday, and she was just fine. If it's not Gree (her name for my mother) there are several other candidates in this family. So let me see what's going on."

Marc's calls in on the other line.

"I'll call you back, sweetheart," I say and answer Marc's call.

Coming in hot once again, I initiate the conversation without a hello. "Okay, what the hell is going on with my family? Meggie just called me. She said Ruthie's dead?"

"Honey, I'm so sorry, but it's true. I talked to Karen. She's with Marian, Timmy, and Ray at Ruthie's condo. She's gone," he says.

"Ruthie?! My sister Ruthie? What the hell happened?" I asked. It's still not registering.

"She took her own life," he states.

"Hold up! Did you just say suicide? Ruthie? Suicide? Ruthie? Are you sure? I'm calling Karen. I'll call you back," I say, stunned.

Now I'm even more confused. There is a mistake. She's a therapist for Christ's sake. She's into all that hippie dippy shit – meditation, Ashrams, self-help books, journaling, sound baths. Her voice mail message literally has instructions on what to do if you're thinking of harming yourself. He must have misheard her. Meggie's wrong. This isn't happening.

I call Karen.

Sr. Karen immediately picks up and proceeds to fill in the details. Recounting the past few days, as family was still in town for Rachel's wedding. There were lunches, dinners, and JoAnne was staying with her. Ruthie dropped her off at the airport on Wednesday morning. JoAnne said she was fine. *Oh, poor JoAnne! Ruthie is like a daughter to her.*

Then, when she didn't call her husband, who stayed in Florida at their winter home, for over 24 hours, he asked Karen to go over to the condo, and they found her with the help of the fire department.

It was true. Karen wouldn't lie. She's a nun. Ruthie died by suicide.

"How? Did she leave a note?" I say. My mind can't process this.

"Pills, it appears," Karen says in her soft, low, 'it's going to be okay' nun voice. The one that makes you feel safe and secure but confirms that this is, in fact, true. *Oh, poor Karen! She just lost her sister, but here she is being a Sister. She's heartbroken. I can tell.*

"Yes, she left a Post-it," she said.

The note stated, 'I just can't do this life anymore.'"

I hang up.

It's true.

Am I in the Twilight Zone? A Post-it? I say in my best Carrie Bradshaw voice.

There was no *King Lear* howl like when I lost Marty. Instead, Pearl Jam's "Porch" starts playing in my head:

What the fuck is this world

Running to...

Shell-shocked. I shut down my computer, gather my things, walk into my boss, Val's, office, and in a choked-up voice mixed with a hint of disbelief, say, "I need to go. My sister Ruthie has killed herself. I'm not sure what's going on. I'll call you when I know more. I have to go. I can barely process this."

Val hugs me. We've worked together for almost a decade. We're close, and she knows my family.

"Are you sure you're okay to drive?" she says.

"Yes, I need to get to Meggie. Ruthie is like a second mom to her," I say. "We just saw her Saturday at Rachel's wedding. What is happening? !!?!?? I need to go. Can you call Meggie and tell her I'm on my way?"

Meggie is living with her boyfriend in her childhood home on Lake Road. 25 -35 minutes away. On my way there, I call Heather as reality starts to sink-in. She's equally as stunned. *Ruthie?* Now I've said it out loud. I hang up, find "Ten" in my CD magazine and turn it up "Porch" as loud as it will go.

I finally reach Meg. Ten minutes later. Heather showed up on our porch. Booze and friendship in hand. Ready to pick up the pieces. The rest of that day was and still is a blur.

The next thing I remember is Marc waiting at my bedside with a mug of Irish Coffee the following day. I had slept past noon. It was true. She was gone. The phone rings. It's Michelle.

"I'm coming to Cleveland. My parents are driving up here, and we're going to travel together out of TPA," she says.

"Yes, of course you can all stay at my house," I reply. "This is unbelievable. Right? Ruthie?" She completely agrees.

I make my way downstairs and thank Marc for the coffee. He knows me so well – I fix another. I let him know that we're about to have houseguests, and we start making a list of things we need to "entertain." I'll never forget Marc going to our bar cabinet, holding up a nearly empty bottle of Jameson and saying, "We're almost out of Whiskey. You better get the big bottles," aka handles. He knows it's going to be a long week.

The phone rings. It's Meggie. She's crushed. I have no answers for her. All I can say is: "Come on out. I'm about to go to Giant Eagle. Michelle, Pat, and Jim are arriving tomorrow and staying here. We can order some Bubba Qs later."

She then informs me that Russ and Andy were wondering what was going on today. The siblings were gathering at Jerry's. "Have you talked to anyone?" she asks. "Nope, news to me!" I reply.

Just then, Rachel calls. I don't answer, but quickly realize people are looking to me for an answer and what to do next. I'm the link to the siblings, and as the oldest granddaughter, hold a bit of rank with the cousins. Plus, I have a big enough house to hold everyone with the tranquility of a Lake Erie as the backdrop—visible from every room in my house. It's my time to lead.

I start putting a plan together. My family needs me. And I thrive in chaos. I can be the anchor we all need right now. I decide, Bubba-Qs at my house tonight (*and no, you can't bring anything*). Then I'll orchestrate all of us getting together here tomorrow night. Marc and I will take care of the main food, and I'll assign side-dishes, beverages, and ice. All are welcome, yes, this includes my mom. We had been estranged for a few years at that point.

My message: "We don't want the first time we see each other to be at the funeral home. I'll discuss it with all the cousins tonight and start spreading the word to the siblings." See, problem-solving is my superpower.

I suddenly remember, I need to cancel all of our travel plans! We already missed our flight. Thank God for travel insurance. No amount of planning in the world could have foreseen this. Ruthie? That was not on my Bingo card.

That night, we started openly talking about Bruno as we were trying to figure out how Ruthie, of all people, died by suicide. No joking, no "crazy talk", no shame. It was a very raw and powerful discussion about mental health.

We all knew that Ruthie, like many of us, it turns out, was on antidepressants, had anxiety, etc. But Ruthie? She was our North Star. She was the one you called for advice. That was literally her job.

We started working on the puzzle. Trading stories of our interactions with her at the wedding. Nothing out of the ordinary. Nothing that would signal this! But the more we talked, the more we realized that the signs were all there. We just didn't know how to recognize them. Because *we don't talk about Bruno.*

For the first time, I understood that dying by suicide is not about selfishness, weakness, drug addiction, or nervous break-downs. It was about a pain so bad she just wanted it to stop.

That week, I went from telling Marty's middle son, Brian, when he arrived that night: "When your father died, I thought I experienced the worst pain I ever could. I was wrong."

To: "What pains me the most is that she was in that much pain. That she saw no other way out."

Somewhere between those two sentences, something in me shifted—from judgment I didn't know I had, to compassion I didn't know I needed.

I couldn't see it because I just couldn't wrap my head around that level of pain.

Until the day I tried to live.

Chapter 12:
Drive

"All the rusted signs we ignore
throughout our lives
Choosing the shiny ones instead."
—*Pearl Jam, "*Thumbing My Way*"*

AMPA IS AN hour away from Tampa, meaning that even the closest destinations can take forever. Traffic is no joke in this town. So when I tell people that I live in Palm Harbor and work in Ybor City, 25 miles apart, they act like I'm commuting from Mars. They look at me like I'm some sort of Martian, too. Although many Clevelanders won't cross the Cuyahoga River from the east side to the west side, Tampaians take travel boundaries to a whole new level.

People in this town won't travel "north" of certain *streets* or even travel from one neighboring city to the next that is less than 6 miles away. It amazes me how many people can't even be bothered to travel to the beach.

Truth is, a lot of times, I don't mind my commute. I do some of my best thinking in the car--*well, there was that one time when thinking got dangerous.* I can blare the music, decompress from my day, listen to an audiobook or catch up with a friend. Often with the top down on my Jeep. Plus, I get to drive over water and see dolphins, pelicans, and at certain times of the year, amazing sunrises and sunsets.

The irony is that my anxiety has long been tied to driving. It began in childhood, when my mother's car was T-boned on the passenger side. I fractured my arm, hit my head, and spent another night alone in the hospital for observation. Turning sixteen in the winter and learning to drive in the snow didn't help. Marty's death in an automobile accident only reinforced what my body already knew.

At one point my panic attacks were so severe that I couldn't drive on a main road. Highways were out of the question. So, this is taking forever to get a few miles, not a big deal. Overcoming my fear of driving was one of my first experiences with therapy.

Somewhere along the way, the car stopped being just a way to get from point A to point B. It became a place where I paid attention. I had to regain control of my emotions and quell the panic. Breathe.

One afternoon, on my way home from work, I noticed a rusted van right next to me. Thankfully, traffic had slowed to a crawl because there was so much to take in. This van had seen some shit!

It was an old Volkswagen bus—low to the ground, long past its prime. Nearly every single inch of this van was rusted. There was not one speck of paint left on this vehicle. Its only color could be found in the faded travel stickers adorning the back windows. Its only shine came from the VW emblem embedded in the front nose panel.

But this vehicle didn't come from the rust belt. Its deep, rusted red-brown hue was sun-soaked and ocean salt-kissed, not smog-damaged and road salt-kissed. It belonged to someone who loved to travel into the wild. A road-trip van that had a thousand stories to tell.

As traffic eased up and the expressway split, I went one way and the van went the other. Off on its next adventure, I imagined.

After years of running in place on a dreadmill, staring out over frozen Lake Erie and dreaming of somewhere else, I found myself running on a beach. When I moved to Florida, I took up running on causeways and bridges—nature's gym.

Living on the Gulf Coast, in Tampa Bay—a peninsula inside a peninsula—there's no shortage of options. Closest to my home is the three-mile Dunedin Causeway, stretched between the Intracoastal Waterway on one side and the Gulf of Mexico on the other. Narrow beaches flank both sides of the road, water meeting land in a way that feels expansive rather than confining.

The causeway leads to a state park, called Honeymoon Island, preserving this precious strip of land from restaurants, high rises, and hotels that have invaded many of Florida's sleepy beachfront towns. The Dunedin Causeway is largely a place for locals, and my favorite place to spend time and exercise on the weekends.

Then what to my wondering eyes should appear, but the van I spotted on 1-75 this week in traffic. The rusted one. Just sitting there. Parked in the sand. It's driver staring out into water so blue it seems endless. I couldn't believe it! I was in the middle of a run, so I just snapped a quick picture.

When I got home, I posted the picture on Facebook captioning it "when the lyric from your favorite Pearl Jam song shows up in person twice in one week, you wonder what it is trying to tell you."

It wasn't until I fully assembled my glam squad, started opening myself to others, and began writing this book that I began to understand its meaning.

This is not a road-trip fantasy van.

It's a survived-some-things van.

A van that's been broken in, not broken down.

A van that kept going.

A van that looks like it knows something about waiting, about arriving, about staying put long enough to be seen.

It doesn't sparkle—but it belongs on the cover of a book called *Champagne & Hashbrowns* because it understands both.

Chapter 13:
Assemble Your Glam Squad

IT TOOK A global shutdown for me to realize I'd been emotionally quarantined for years. That—and thinking about driving off a bridge.

Florida isolation hit differently. The palm trees looked like freedom, but the silence echoed like punishment. I'd built a life where "I've got it" was both my motto and my prison. From the outside, I looked steady—career intact, smile polished, makeup on even for Zoom. Inside, I was running on fumes and caffeine, chasing whatever sparkled loudest and promised relief from a restlessness I couldn't name.

I was performing that survival publicly while hosting a book launch in my office—written by a woman I admired, someone who had turned pain into purpose. I'd hosted plenty of signings over the years. I always found inspiration in them. I also quietly wondered if I could ever be one of them. *If only.*

Cue the soundtrack. Ignite the self-doubt. Paste on the smile.

That night, someone finally asked the question that cut through my curated calm.

"So, what fucked you up?"

The question came from a woman named Sharon. That's right, another Sharon, which, let's be honest, already felt like a cosmic joke—*Two Sharons are better than two Karens, right?* (apologies to those poor unfortunate souls named Karen).

She was one of the first people I met in Florida, and it had been a while since we had seen each other. My initial thought was,

"Great, someone I can hang with and have an actual dialogue with." I was not in the mood for the usual small talk. Plus, she had been on my mind. I took it as a sign.

I immediately vibed with the other Sharon. She was bold, fashionable, fabulous—she'd even been on *Say Yes to the Dress*. During the pandemic, she wrote a book about her struggles with addiction. It was raw, unfiltered, and brave. I admired how she told the truth out loud. She had this uncanny ability to make you laugh and flinch at the same time, as she'd already done the work you were still avoiding.

Since starting therapy, I'd been writing quietly again—but only as therapy, not testimony. Her book made me wonder if I could do the same.

A few weeks later, we met for breakfast. I told her about the bridge moment—the panic, the therapy, the PTSD, the resentment, the restlessness, my unfulfilled dreams, my mother, and the exhaustion of holding it all together. *It was a two-hour breakfast.*

She didn't try to fix it. She didn't say "same." She didn't ask me, "Have you ever read or tried?" She listened and then simply said, "So, hire me. And I want you to *ask me* for help. It's an important first step. Ask me to help you with the one thing holding you back - you!"

I asked. I became her client. It felt radical—like permission to finally invest in my own healing. It was a bold step. Yes, I was paying a therapist, but I'd never paid someone to help me, face-to-face, one-on-one, professionally.

To be my coach.

That was the part that scared me. Paying meant I couldn't pretend I was "working on it." I couldn't half-try and blame the process when nothing changed. I had to show up—honestly, consistently, and without an exit ramp.

"Old Sharon" turned to books, many half-read, courses started and abandoned, and experts admired from a safe distance. I convinced myself I was doing the work, but like everything else, it wasn't working! (*because I'm flawed*). I was just trying to DIY myself out and find a quick fix. Just like you can't exercise your way out of a bad diet, you can't DIY yourself out of pain. I'd spent money in all the wrong places and called it growth.

When Sharon F. told me her fee, I didn't hesitate. Not because it was cheap—it wasn't—but because for the first time, I believed someone could actually help me. Something had to give.

I didn't know it then, but that moment was the beginning of assembling my glam squad.

I'd always thought a glam squad was for Housewives—the kind with spray tans, contour kits, and assistants named Blaire. Turns out, it's for survival. A glam squad isn't vanity; it's infrastructure.

Starting over professionally also meant starting over socially— and that hit a much deeper nerve than I expected. One thing I failed to foresee when I blew up my career in my forties was that I'd have to rebuild *my entire professional network*. Sure, I had the skills and experience, but I no longer had the luxury of knowing everyone in town.

Since fundraising is built on relationships, Houston, this was a problem.

Turns out, this was harder than I expected. Like champagne and hashbrowns, I can make connections with people. Once I do, it's magic. Getting there, though, kicks my anxiety into overdrive. In my mind, at work Sharon, and at home, Sharon lives two very different lives. And I only give my work "friends" a small glimpse into my real homelife.

Sharon F. and I met through a networking group called

Working Women of Tampa Bay (WWTB). Unlike other professional groups where membership is based on status or title, WWTB welcomed everyone. It was filled with women like me—starting over, starting out, and genuinely rooting for each other. This wasn't about friendship. It was about building support from scratch, without history to hide behind.

I didn't really give much thought to having to make new friends, either. I had family and an old high school friend here. I was good. I wasn't without love. I was without proximity, and I just didn't know how to ask for help *where I was.*

I've had the same core friends since childhood. Heather, Margaret, Lisa, and now sometimes my daughter, Meghanne (the squirrel wrangler). Barb is in the mix too, though that one's... complicated.

Margaret came first. We met when we were four. Her mom was friends with my grandmother. When I returned to OLA in fourth grade, Barb came with Margaret, and Heather—the new girl in sixth grade—tricked me into our friendship with a ruse about a broken curling iron. *Remember, I don't take to new people well.*

It was the age of corded phones, big hair, and blue eye shadow. Heather phoned me up in a panic. We had cheerleading tryouts in an hour, and I lived the closest to her. Could she please come over and finish getting ready? I may not make friends easily, but I'm your girl in a crisis and always willing to help someone in need.

That's all it took. We became inseparable.

Following tryouts (we both made the squad), we went to Heather's house. Upon hearing my last name, her mom asked if I was related to Ruth and Ray Somerville. "I'm their grand-daughter," I replied.

She proceeded to tell me the following story:

"I met your grandparents at a wedding. We arrived 45

minutes late, dinner being already served. After apologizing to the entire table for being so late, blaming it on being pregnant and trying to get out of the house with the mayhem of four children, I sat down next to your grandmother.

When I asked her if she had any children, she calmly said, 'Yes, nine, and I'm pregnant with number ten.' We laughed so hard."

She continued, "Good people, your grandparents. You look like her. Such a tragedy. Sit down. "Are you hungry?"

That's all it took. I was forever welcome.

A few days later, Heather and I ventured into her basement, where I discovered a full-service styling salon, complete with a shampoo bowl, style chair, and a variety of curling irons. Turns out her mother was a hairdresser as well and did clients in their home! Perplexed, Heather confessed she thought I was a cool girl and just wanted to get to know me. I wasn't mad. I gave her a high five and mad props. It's not easy to fool me.

Lisa joined later, via Mr. Video, the neighborhood arcade, and the Catholic Youth Organization (CYO) cheerleading tournaments. Her parish—St. Pat's, West Park—hosted the big CYO tournament. They always won. Hmm.

By high school, we all converged at St. Joseph Academy (SJA), a girls' school set on a campus worthy of Hogwarts. The OLA girls ruled the court, if for no other reason than SJA was in OLA parish. The legendary Walk of Roses is a tradition in which seniors dressed in white caps and gowns walk down the middle of Rocky River Drive between the two locations, carrying a dozen red roses each to their commencement ceremony. If you are not familiar, I encourage you to Google a video. There is nothing like a group of educated women taking to the streets on their way to change the world. Hmm.

I didn't have to wait until college to experience something

like a sorority. Good thing, because last I checked, there isn't one for moms. We were the popular crowd, sure—but more sisterhood with a side of snark. Long before *Mean Girls* became a movie, we were already proof that belonging could be powerful without being cruel.

These are my ride-or-dies, my truth-tellers, and my grounding force. We talk every day, primarily through group text, which is always in the middle of several conversations since we live in different time zones. There is nothing off-limits in this group, and no joke is too irreverent.

We can go from discussing a very serious health or family issue topic to dropping a hilarious TikTok or meme right in the middle of the thread without question, judgement or concern about timing.

We all come from big West Park families—the kind fueled by alcoholism, Catholic guilt, and more unspoken trauma than any of us could untangle. Talk about trauma bonding. We were raised on the same streets, in the same pews, by parents who shared the same hangovers. Our siblings all knew each other's siblings; some even married into other families. At this point, I'm not sure where one family ends, and another begins.

Heather is married to Margaret's older brother, and Margaret's husband is my first husband's best friend. We love each other's kids like they're our own. And now our adult children are friends with their own relationships. It's not messy. It's family. *Ohana.*

Sharon F. and I bonded over unexpected things, too—like The Real Housewives of Beverly Hills. It came up casually at our first meeting, almost as a joke.

She said, "It could be worse. You could be like them."

What? What?

I kind of wanted that life.

Growing up in a salon, I was raised on *National Enquirer*, *Cosmopolitan*, and *People* magazine—which, by the way, still shows up in my mailbox and gets read religiously every week. Glamour wasn't frivolous—it was aspirational. Glam squads. Fabulous clothes. Birkin bags. Private jets. Big houses. Staff. Assistants. Their lives looked amazing. Effortless. Protected.

Sharon didn't see it that way at all. To her, it was work. Manufactured drama. A job built on performance, not real intimacy. Not real friendship. She watched it as a guilty pleasure, with distance. I watched it like a fantasy. That difference mattered.

It made me realize how much of what I'd been chasing wasn't success or balance—because work–life balance is a myth. Balance implies symmetry. What most of us are actually doing is triage—deciding what gets dropped so we can keep moving.

Work and life aren't opposites; they coexist, messy and imperfect, like champagne and hashbrowns. And if I'm going to build something big, I need support that understands both.

A few years back, career development circles loved the phrase personal board of directors—the idea that instead of one mentor, you surround yourself with smart people who offer guidance, perspective, and accountability.

My version is a glam squad. Not because it's cute, but because it's honest. This isn't just about career advice or strategy. It's about having people who help you show up in your whole life— professionally, personally, emotionally—without pretending those things can be separated.

Same concept. Different language.

Everyone's glam squad looks different because everyone's needs are different. Mine includes people I pay and people I don't—and I don't apologize for that. My therapist. My business coach. My doctor. My pool service. My grocery delivery service. My daughter. The West Park Coven. My grant writer. My work team. My cheerleaders. My lash artist. My Disney +1 (aka the Other Meg) , etc.

Together, they form a carefully built ecosystem that supports who I am and what I'm building—lightening the load of tasks that once triggered anxiety and reminding me I don't have to do everything alone. In the end, it wasn't about finding a new version of me. It was about remembering the one who'd been buried under all that survival—the girl who believed in second chances, in showing up, in rebuilding from rubble. The one who still believed in hope, trust, and a little pixie dust.

Self-respect isn't a makeover.

It's management.

It's strategy.

It's choosing the people and systems that help me show up as my highest, truest self.

Sharon F. and Dr. B. helped me see that glossing over what happened—thinking about driving off a bridge—wasn't just a bad day. It meant I didn't want to be here. That mattered. A lot.

Sharon asked what I was doing for me—not as a caregiver or crisis manager, but as a person carrying a load that heavy. I didn't have an answer beyond manicures and pedicures.

Later, I mentioned an upcoming trip to New York to see *Othello* on Broadway. She looked confused—until I told her I was a Shakespearean scholar.

"What?!" she said. "That's a plot twist I did not see coming. I would start every conversation with that."

People never see that one coming. Kinda like driving with a Christmas Tree in your convertible. But for a long time, I thought it was because it didn't fit me. I wasn't good enough, and it's one of my unfinished projects. But I came to realize the reason people were surprised by this statement had nothing to do with me. It is just a generally unexpected statement. I mean, how often do you hear "I'm a Shakespearean scholar?" I'll wait. I certainly don't say "me too!" that often. *Something Special.*

No really. I'm a book nerd. Do you believe it? I've been pulling this line out as a party trick for years, especially during the dreaded corporate icebreaker activities. *God, I hate forced networking.*

But she helped me see it differently—not as a novelty, but as something essential. Shakespeare. The original word master. The original drama king. The most quoted writer in history. It was unique and uniquely me.

Something shifted. Maybe I wasn't a mistake after all. Maybe I wasn't broken. Maybe I'd just forgotten who I was before survival took over.

My glam squad didn't save me.

They reminded me I was worth saving.

Part 4:
Grit & Grace with a Side of Glitter

Chapter 14:
Champagne and Hashrowns
Side A

Here's to those who lost and loved.
Here's to those who are looking
down on us from above.
Aye. Aye.
--Somerville Family Toast

"SO, HOW WAS the weekend? How was Chicago? How was the show?" I heard coming across the parking lot as I climbed out of my car.

Damn it! I was really hoping to get in the door, go straight to my office, shut the door, and address whatever fresh hell was awaiting me in my email after a few PTO days.

I couldn't ignore her. We were going through the same locked door; she would get there first to turn the key, and she was one of those chatty morning people. Plus, she was my boss.

I tried to get away with a grey-rock, monotone answer, "It was great." But my concert-strained, sleep-deprived, barely-there voice was telling a different story.

"Sounds like it was more than great?!?," she said excitedly. "Put your stuff down and come to my office. I want to hear all about it!"

Boom! And there it was. Ugh.

"Okay, Sharon," I said to myself as I dropped my keys, purse, *"Pull yourself together, take a deep breath, and put on that*

game face. Next time, don't share your anticipation and excitement so much, and people won't ask you questions."

I confidently walked into my boss's office. "Do you watch the show 'Shameless?'" my raspy voice eked out as I made my way to the office guest chair. I could tell by her face that she didn't.

"Well, let's just say my weekend could have been an episode on that show. For starters, I came home penniless, with two black eyes, and it was still the best weekend of my life!" I said with a chuckle as I took off my sunglasses. "I covered it the best I could."

"OMG! Are you okay? What happened!?" she inquired as she put her hand over her open mouth.

"Yeah, I'm fine. I was pick-pocketed on the L after the show. It was dumb, really. I knew it the minute it happened. I had a cross-body bag on, but it wasn't zipped. The train was packed with people from the show. And I'm not gonna lie, I started off my day with champagne and hashbrowns, that rolled right into the concert, and there were post-show libations. There were many of us on the L heading out. We were still all singing Pearl Jam and having a great time. Then as the L hard stopped at my exit, this dude bummed into me while he reached down into my open bag and grabbed my slim fit wallet. I felt and saw it happen. That sobered me up right quick and I chased after that mother fucker. I mean after all I did have combat boots on, but I got tripped up on the turnstile, fell and scrapped my knees and the hand that broke my fall." I held up my road rashed hand to show her.

I continued: "But that's not how I got the black eyes. That happened after a harrowing morning of trying to figure out how the hell I was going to get on the plane without an ID. Long story short, you must make an official police report. The hotel vouched for my identify because they saw my driver's license when I checked in. I then took a copy of said police report to TSA where they took me in one of those 'come with me' rooms and practically strip searched me. I barely made my plane. In my haste and exhaustion, coupled with a banged-up hand, I overshot the overhead bin and my suitcase fell right back on my nose. Hence the black eyes," I paused, laughed and said, "But, still the BEST weekend ever!"

Although she pressed me for more details, she *was* my boss. I quickly ended the conversation by saying, "Pearl Jam at Wrigley was obviously amazing. Heather and I *always* have fun together. We'll be laughing about this weekend for a really long time. I'll fill you in at some point, but I need to get to work before my boss comes looking for me," I said with my expertly timed GenX self-deprecating humor.

She had beaten me out for the top job that we both were competing for. Being a former Executive Director, I may have had a leg up on the experience side, but she had home-field advantage. Like a first runner-up in a beauty pageant, I was just happy to be sharing the stage, and it got me to Florida. So, in my mind. I did take home the crown.

We were going to be a "team"—two women finally stepping into our own – rising above the hands of micromanaging that were holding us down. We'd both seen the seedy underbelly. We knew what needed to change, knew there was going to be a big learning curve for the board, as it was smoke and mirrors before us. It was going to be a lot of work. However, we were up to the challenge!

Still, from day one, there was always an air of foreboding and anxiety to perform. Like many nonprofits they expected miracles from their Development Director, especially their first one, with a proven track record of philanthropy. Nonprofits are always expected to do more with less, achieve more than before and the need always outpaces the funding. There hasn't been one job in my career that didn't start already behind due to the staffing gap I was filling. Something, and sometimes, everything, was on fire. Runways to success were short but I always managed to save the day. I am Batman after all. However, this quick hit of success (like a perfectly pulled off fundraising that was just weeks away with barely anything done yet or tackling the uncollected pledges that brought immediate cash flow) often created an unreal expectation for things to come. Real philanthropy takes time.

Sure, they had special events with big money donors and a healthy number of surprise bequests each year (something I would learn is characteristic of sector of philanthropy). However, they certainly didn't have an annual fund, leading to a major gifts program, which then turn into transformational funds, and finally reaching pinnacle of the donor cycle— Planned Gifts. And, because these gifts were on the larger end (once received one for $8M), they were more than subsiding the P&L to make ends meet. Although you could chip away at that nut over time, it was a big mountain to climb and certainly wasn't going to happen in my first year. But apparently, that is what I signed up for; I failed to ask all the right questions before saying yes. Needless to say, it didn't go well. Nor did my move to Florida.

My move to Florida had not gone according to plan, primarily because I didn't have a very good one to begin with. I had a YOLO, failure is not an option, attitude backed by my motto "problem solving is my superpower." After all, all the planning in the world didn't prevent Ruthie's death from upsetting my meticulously planned Florida trip. Life will get you no matter what. So far, my life had been filled with grief, abuse, trauma and course correcting that I thought if I'm going to be in so much pain, at least I could do it somewhere where it was sunny. I didn't think I could make it through another grey winter in Cleveland. Plus, if Ruthie's death taught me anything, it was that life was happening right now. No time like the present. I wanted to LIVE the life I always dreamed of in Florida not be a retiree in God's waiting room. I had like at least 25+ years until retirement and because I've worked in non-profit my whole life, it's not like I had a huge pension waiting for me anyways.

So, I set my sights on finding a job in Florida and the rest would follow. Marc, my gotta promise not to stop when I say when husband, was on board with this plan until it became a reality. The night of my going away soiree he informed me that he really didn't want to go and I could probably get my Cleveland job back. He really loved our home on Lake Erie (it was spectacular), his neurologist (he was amazing), and his roots (friends, family, and familiarity). He had some pretty sound arguments, but he was as resolute in staying as I was in going. A stalemate ensued. I went anyways and it took nearly two years for him to join me. Add that to the baggage I'm bringing to this new job.

By the time the Pearl Jam tour rolled around, the board was turning up the heat and performance anxiety was the general mood in the office. I've felt this vibe before in other offices, that hum of panic just beneath the surface, but didn't quite know what to do with it except work harder. Longer. Louder. My anxiety loves me some 'stress' – it's where I shine!- but it also eats me alive. Slowing. Until my self-esteem, self-worth, and self-doubt are all sitting at the same damn table whispering, *See? It's you.* Self-sabotage then gives way to self-fulfilling prophecy. I end up just spinning my wheels no matter how hard I pedaled. Ending in defeat. I was let go. They wanted to go in a different direction.

It's not unusual for me to attend several shows on one tour. In 35 years, Pearl Jam has never performed the same set list twice. It's part of the fun, especially if you're like me and love chasing white rabbits and white whales. My rabbit: *Thumbing My Way* which at time I'm writing this, it's been 7,179 days since I've seen it live. My whale: *Comes then Goes.* Maybe next show.

I had hoped that Marc would join me on at least one of the four shows that I procured tickets for – three in Florida and Wrigley. Hoping that it would be the spark we needed to move forward, be together, have fun, and get back on track. High hopes as we were barely speaking. For the three Florida shows, he stayed put in Ohio. I sold my extra ticket and went solo. If I could do it at six, I could do it at forty-six.

Wrigley was my last chance. Wrigley is magic. Chicago is magic. We both loved the windy city. Marc did boot camp there and I spent a few weekends there when I was in college. Tina's brother was attending a Chicago law-school and had a place on printer's row. Southwest was new in the market and did these amazing 2-1 deal from CLE to MDW. Chicago was the destination for our first couples' trip to catch the Tribe take on the Cubs, the year interleague play was introduced to MLB.

Still at a stalemate and heading toward the inevitable – another failed marriage and another job loss, Wrigley was going to be my last hurrah before I returned to Florida to figure out what's next. And there was no one else I'd rather share that with than Heather – the one who introduced me to Eddie in the first place. After high school her and a few of my friends took off to the Pacific Northwest to work at a casino, follow the Grateful Dead, and live the kind of wild freedom your twenties are meant for. They were spending time in clubs checking out up-and-coming bands like Soundgarden, Alice in Chains, and Pearl Jam. Basically, they were living the movie *Singles* while I was at home chasing a toddler.

After years of spinning records together, Heather had zero doubt that the sounds coming out of Seattle would be my jam, and so gave me a copy of the *Singles* soundtrack. Heather has always known exactly who I am. Heather has always seen me for exactly who I am.

Naturally, she jumped at the chance to meet me in Chicago to see Pearl Jam. The day before the show, I flew in early, settled into our hotel overlooking Lake Xichigan, and headed up to Wrigleyville to pick up our tickets for the show. Back then, you had to pick up your Ten Club tickets in person with an ID matching your 10CLB membership name. I figured while

I was at it, I was going to pick up some merch. But the lines were insane and instead I spent the afternoon at Murphy's hanging with other Jamily members. I mean, the only lines I wait in are at Disney.

Heather arrived later that night and we immediately hit the town. Without a destination in mind, we came across "Chicago's oldest bar", said the marquis, a place called the Green Door. Irish girls always find the Irish pub. And Irish people from big Catholic families always run into people they know, no matter where they are. This was no exception. Heather's cousins, from Cleveland, were in town for friend's wedding and, of course, ended up at the Green Door after the rehearsal dinner. We promptly joined the group and pissed the night away until last call. While I had the benefit of a power nap after my afternoon at Murphy's, Heather did not. Inebriated, the Drunchies set-in, quick. Luckily just a few doors down was a place called Mr. Beef. "A cozy, little sandwich joint that's been slingin' tasty eats for over 30 years," it says on their website.

I could tell we were in somewhere famous because autographed celebrity photos covered the wall. I perused them like flipping through a *People Magazine* as Heather was ordering her food. There was no chance I was eating here. I have IBS and a Pearl Jam concert tomorrow. The cheese and crackers in the Bento box I picked up at the hotel pantry upon check-in, will do just fine. I also picked up Gatorade, water, candy, Combos, and other "party" supplies. *This isn't my first Rodeo.*

Years later, when *The Bear* blew up, I almost spit out my coffee when I realized it was Mr. Beef coming across my screen.

I immediately texted Heather, "Have you watched 'The Bear' yet?"

Reply: "No, should I?"

Me: "Yes, and call me when you know."

A couple of hours later, my phone rang, "Mr. Beef!!!!" I heard through a roar of laughter.

And damn was that show accurate. Pretty sure during Season 3, Episode 7, the mayonnaise customers are based on our night there. My celebrity gallery viewing was interrupted by Heather "arguing" with the line cook about putting mayo on her order. To de-escalate the situation, I pulled out my FAFO voice and sternly said, "Just put the fucking mayo on the sandwich. It's gross. But she LOVES it."

Mic Drop.

"Yes, Ma'am," he sheepishly replies.

The next morning, I woke up like an excited Disney Adult. Sure, I was hanging, but I knew I could rally. I had a plan. Heather, on the other hand, was hanging hard. I let her sleep as long as I could, but if we were going to turn this thing around, brunch was a must! Once again, we took to the streets of Chicago. It was a glorious August day – I had forgotten how amazing Summer was on the Great Lakes. No humidity. Breezes. No wonder Marc doesn't want to move to Florida, where in August, you are drenched with sweat the minute you walk out the door.

We passed a couple of places that were either closed or near closing. We had a long day ahead of us, we're not rushing this! Then, after peering into a restaurant that had its garage doors open on this glorious day, I declared this was the spot. "They have champagne and hashbrowns! That's all I need!" Apparently, I said this in my Somerville voice, so that whole restaurant heard me.

As we sit down, I can see a large s table of brunch goers laughing. I know it's because of what I just said. I caught their attention. I piqued their interest. That is not something you hear every day, especially said with such confidence.

Our waiter arrives at our table, as Heather visits the water closet, and I promptly order a bottle of Champagne (Moët if you have it – they don't), and hashbrowns. "Can you tell me a little bit about your hashbrowns?" I asked. "They are hashbrowns," he answers awkwardly with a hint of: *is this really a question?* Then I proceeded to recite a cerulean sweater monologue about hashbrowns ala Miranda Priestly in "The Devil Wears Prada." We then come to an agreement on what I will find acceptable.

As he returns to the table with the champagne bucket and two glasses, so does Heather. "I hand him back the second glass. Oh no, honey, that's just for me, I don't know what she wants." In the words of Scar, I mutter under my breath: *I'm surrounded by idiots.* The brunch table snickers in the distance.

At the table next to us sits a single rider wearing an "It doesn't get any Vedder than this" t-shirt. Heather—who's never met a stranger she couldn't gather enough facts about to write their entire memoir—strikes up a conversation.

Here we go again. I do small talk for a living; I have the same friends I've had since grade school, and I've got champagne and hashbrowns. I'm good. *Can't I just enjoy my brunch in peace?*

While they chat, Single Rider turns to me and asks:

"Did you really pick this restaurant because they serve champagne and hashbrowns?"

"Why, yes. Yes, I did," I say, matter-of-factly, and bring the flute to my lip.

Thank goodness they had proper champagne glasses. *Our poor waiter thought he got a schooling about the variety of hashbrowns.* Huh. I'm serious about my glassware. Don't ever try to serve me a Moscow mule in anything but a copper cup. Just ask my friends Chrissie and Kelly about our night at the Hard Rock.

"I don't think I've ever heard anyone do that before. That's... a rather odd combination."

"Not odd," I reply. "Unique. Like me. Last I checked, there's no Champagne police."

What is it with this town? First, you can't put mayo on a steak sandwich, and now this?

Heather, sensing my frustration—and the ache I've been trying to drown in bubbles—turns the conversation back to me.

"So, how's Florida, Sha? What's going on with you and Marc?"

"Nothing good to report. But let's not talk about that now. I'm seeing my Eddie tonight at Wrigley with my very best friend." I raise my glass. "Cheers—to Champagne and Hashbrowns."

From that moment on, Champagne and Hashbrowns became our catch phrase. Our very own: "C'est la vie."

Chapter 15:
Champagne and HashBrowns
Side B

MY TRIP TO Chicago with Heather gave me just enough of a recharge to face some tough facts. This job, this city, and this marriage definitely were not working. Changes needed to be made. Marc and I reopened our dialogue, initially about ending it, but as we began to really listen to each other instead of trying to win, we somehow found a middle ground.

We agreed that we would keep the Lake Erie house and he would move to Florida for one year. We would move to a resort-style apartment on the Tampa Bay, where we had a built-in social circle and activities. If there was one thing I learned in my time here alone, living in Florida and vacationing in Florida were two very different things. And, while I was out there in the world, Marc, retired, needed more than just our golden retriever, Butters, and a screened-in porch. Although maintaining this lifestyle was going to be pricey, the fact remained that we really did love each other enough to give it one last try. We agreed on a year, caught between what was closing and what might rise next—my own quiet version of Pearl Jam's *"Setting Sun."*

We set three non-negotiable ground rules.

1. We would both keep an open mind and recognize that homesickness was normal – *Florida, it's not so bad* was our motto.

2. We would actively participate in our new life – exploring one new thing every week, making friends, and doing more of the things we loved.

3. We would work as a team and make decisions together – No pulling rank, ultimatums, or our usual, fuck it, I'm going to do it anyway. I'm a grown ass adult, and I don't need your permission to live my life! All of this was 100% off the table. That's how we ended up here in the first place.

While all this was proving to be a very handy framework to rebuild our marriage, the angst of restlessness still consumed me, and I continued to fall into all the old patterns. Trying to fix the system by eating the frog, practicing gratitude, tiny magic, scaring my soul, or being a badass. I tried Cycle Bar, Orange Theory, Hot Yoga, etc. Sure, all of these were incredibly helpful, and I made incremental progress, but life's setbacks would knock the wind right out of me, have me crying on the bathroom floor, and ultimately, thinking of driving off a bridge when it just became too much.

The world continued to send me mixed messages as I kept trying to find my career fit in Florida. Still, too loud, too spicy, too outspoken, too direct, and generally too much. Yet at the same time, this was exactly why people thought I was fabulous, and without a doubt, the one who got shit done. Inside, I was literally dying, outside, I was continuing to rebound, rebuild, and check things off my bucket list. Champagne and Hashbrowns.

Trauma therapy started to change that. Instead of going through a list of my issues that I still needed to "deal with," offering a temporary fix to a situational problem. Framework to confront things head-on, apply to the anxiety, depression, and panic that would continue to follow me. By identifying my triggers and really becoming in tune with how they affected my health, wealth, and self. Fixing the symptoms, not fully addressing the causes.

One of the first assignments I was given by my therapist involved...you guessed it... a trip to Wrigley Field to see Pearl Jam. I can't make this shit up.

Although Marc and I were on solid footing and by then had settled into our Florida dream home, he was not.

His MS really was affecting his mobility, and I knew this trip would be a lot of walking, even with taking Uber. Getting there is usually not the problem; it's after the show. Ubers rarely pick up right at the gate after a show; it's typically a few blocks away. That's hard enough for Marc even on a good day, let alone after we'd been singing, dancing, and drinking for a 26-song set-list. This would mean I'd have to be on high alert all night. The night would often end in frustration and arguing, tainting the whole experience. *Wasn't I allowed to ever have a good time? Why do I always have to carry the load?*

Since we were doing both the Thursday and Saturday night shows, this was going to be tough. To up the ante, I had secured FRONT ROW seats for night two. Now our days of Standing Room only General Admission tickets are long gone, but Pearl Jam did something really special for Wrigley. They put two ADA sections with seating right at the rail! Front row, baby! This would be a first in all the years I've seen this band. I wasn't missing this!

Although I didn't get them in the 10CLB fan lottery, I used the annual bonus I earned by exceeding my goals to buy those seats. They were a mortgage payment.

Side note, I did let the club know that there were nefarious people out there making big money off these seats reserved and intended for **disabled fans**. Not that they could do anything about it, but this is a band that cares about its fans and the world in general. If there was anyone who could prevent this in the future, or at least minimize it, it was them. After all, this is the band that tried to take on Ticketmaster by filing an antitrust complaint against them with the Department of Justice in 1994.

They lost, were called "cute" by a congresswoman (literally), and told to go on their merry way.

They didn't. Pearl Jam has spent the last 30 years trying to find a way to change the system.

Plus, I just couldn't let it go. Me and my big mouth will always point this kind of shit out. Sometimes loudly. Sometimes quietly. While some may call this kind of behavior capitalism, I call it equity.

At first, I did my usual. Over plan and overcompensate. Kicking my anxiety and all its glorious symptoms (depression, irritability, outbursts of anger, foggy brain, resentment, insomnia, stomach problems, etc.) into high gear. Here we go again. *See, even with therapy, I'm a failure. You're just wired this way. You'll never change.*

Then a funny thing happened. My therapist asked me, "Sharon, what would your weekend look like without trying to control your anxiety?"

I told her about all the plans and precautions I was taking. I was giving it my all. I was doing the best I could.

She replied, "You didn't answer my question. You told me about all the ways that you were going to compartmentalize things and look on the bright side. I asked, 'What would your life look like without always trying to control your anxiety?'"

I paused for a moment, and just like when I told Marty about my teenage pregnancy, I told her, "Honestly, I have no idea. I'm a mess, and isn't that what you are for?" *Duh. Thought my trauma was the root cause here. Another waste of time. See, it is you.*

I was so confused. Wasn't that what I was doing? Wasn't that what I've always been doing? Finding ways to control my anxiety?

What I still couldn't see then was that healing didn't mean "fixing" and it certainly doesn't mean "forgetting."

"Okay, well then, I'd like you to make a study of yourself this weekend. You've told me you love to learn, and from what I can tell, it's usually in the pursuit of validation. So, let's make an objective study of you. I want you to pay attention to your moments of frustration, joy, anxiety, etc. You don't have to do anything except pause, breathe, and make a mental note of the circumstances. I want you to slow down, even if it's just for a minute, and really feel in the moment. Pay attention to how you feel physically and mentally," she said.

I responded suspiciously, "Okay...I'll give it a try," thinking with my brain fog of late, I'd better at least jot down a few notes, and added Post-It Notes to my packing list. There was a hint of skepticism in my voice. But no eye roll or sigh of resignation; *here we go again.*

Her question genuinely piqued my curiosity. I wondered.

Debra started our next session. "So, how was the weekend? How was Chicago?"

"A-b-s-o-l-u-t-e-l-y   Ah-ma-zing!"   I   enthusiastically proclaimed.

"I was given a Tambourine from the one and only Eddie Vedder, we made eye contact, and he flashed me the Jeep sign." Still exhilarated, I added, "I still can't believe this is my life."

"That's great, but let's unpack my assignment and what you observed this weekend," she said.

Kill joy.

We talked about the highs (seeing our good friends Robyn

and Josh) and the lows of the weekend (Uber proved to be a challenge). During that discussion, I told her about a picture my husband took of me.

"Now you have to understand that we have a running joke in our family, that when Marc is taking your picture, it will be the worst picture you've ever taken." *Hey now.*

"So, no pressure, but this was a once-in-a-lifetime photo. I was decked out in Daisy Duke jean shorts, my PJ Scotland t-shirt, flannel around my waist, and my fabulous Betsey Johnson combat boots. Every inch of these babies is embellished in rhinestones and pearls in a skull pattern only she could make look chic. These boots sparkle like a disco ball that's seen some things. 1000% me. Grunge glam to a tee. But, with his poor camera skills and my poor body image, this was asking a lot."

"Guess what, he nailed it! I couldn't believe it."

Well done, honey! I was giddy. This was going right on my Facebook profile picture, captured "Pearl Jam Front Row - Dream Come True."

And that's when it hit me—there it was. Me.

The rusted sign I'd been ignoring all my life.

Marc saw me. He perfectly captured the incandescence that is my essence.

It wasn't about the cool experience. It wasn't about checking things off my bucket list. It wasn't just that I was starting to feel comfortable in my own skin.

It was joy.

Sure, I could nit-pick this picture to death, focusing on every minor flaw in my appearance. *What was I thinking wearing those shorts at my age and weight? Or my hair? That double chin!*

And I thought, *oh*

This is what my life without anxiety could look like? Safe, secured, loved, happy? Oh, this is what it feels like? This is what it feels like when you work on healing your trauma, and you really start loving yourself.

I recognized that I didn't need more time in my day; I needed to create more space to see the real me. For the first time, I saw myself as others did, and for the first time in a very long time, I saw light.

See, I told you Wrigley was magic.

Chapter 16:
Rearview Mirror

"I took a drive today, time to emancipate."
—Pearl Jam, "Rearview Mirror"

THE TEXT SIMPLY read "Jake Gyllenhaal and Denzel Washington. WE MUST GO!" It was accompanied by a screenshot of an equally simple graphic, a black box with white lettering that said: "Sign up now at Othellobway.com."

As quickly as my brain processed the thought, *"Hell Yeah! We Must Go!"* My phone was already searching Insta for the *Othello* handle in Meggie's text.

@VedderGirl216 (my Insta handle, of course) was amongst the first 872 people to like the post, and the 26th person to comment: "100% (emoji) will be there!!"

Not. One. Thought. was given to when it was, how much it would cost, or how I was going to make all the logistics work. I just knew I needed to be in the room when it happened. New York City was the destination for our next mother-daughter trip. And this was going to be one for the books!

Our mother-daughter trips started after her dad and me split up. During our eight-year marriage, we had enjoyed at least one annual family vacation to destinations like the Somerville cabin in Tidioute, Pennsylvania, the Outer Banks, Virginia Beach, and, thanks to the generosity of my in-laws, even an all-expense paid trip to Disney World in Florida.

Although our family was going to look different now, this was part of the childhood experience I wanted her to have, and I protected it even as I remarried and took on bonus children. Certain family traditions would be just ours. Or, a blend of a few I wanted to hang onto from mine. Like picking out the Christmas tree in my convertible with the top down, regardless of the Cleveland winter weather. I mean, isn't that why cars came with heaters? If we could sit at Cleveland Browns stadium for three hours on a Sunday in December, we could drive to one of my childhood Christmas Tree lots in West Park, pick out a Blue Spruce, swing through the drive-through at the Kamm's Corner Steak and Shake, ride past the old house on Allien, and flash the peace sign to all the disbelieving onlookers.

It was fun, memorable, and made a statement. This is who we are. Uniquely fabulous and unconventional. *'Tis the season to sparkle and spread joy.*

Even as a teenager, Meggie wasn't like "Mom, this is embarrassing, or why do we have to do this, this is stupid." After all, I was the "cool mom," the one who took her to 'NYSNC at the Cleveland Browns Stadium and then Justin solo years later his Sexy Back, 20/20, Man of the Woods, etc. tours. So, for the most part, she went along with my "traditions" without complaint, and as she got older, the perks and vacations got even better.

I, however, shouldn't be surprised that we're so sympatico, our birthdays are just one day apart, after all – classic Capricorns.

Me: "If you wanted your own birthday. You didn't have to wait until 8:26 a.m., 12:01 a.m. would have been just fine!"

Meg: "Well, if you didn't insist on having your own birthday, heaven forbid you would have to share anything, Mom."

Me: "Hey kiddo, you almost tried to kill me!" I'd retort as we trail off into laughter and continued reminiscing about how I was in the hospital for four days recovering from her birth due to excessive blood loss complicated by anemia.

Even in the late 80s, women with insurance were going home

after one day, akin to the time of a full-day at a hotel – check in at 4:00 p.m. – check out at 11:00 a.m., noon if you request a late check-out. Complete bullshit.

This was also at a time when visiting hours and the visitors themselves were restricted. Immediate family only between the hours of x and y. I'll always fondly recall the nurse telling me my father was here to see the baby. I replied: "Oh, this should be interesting. We've never met." Imagine the look that conjured. It was Ray, of course. My brother Marty also posed as my father so he could see Meggie in the recovery room. This was our baby after all. She promptly shits on him. *Paybacks bro.*

While we each had our own days, January birthdays are the absolute worst. Everyone's broke, on a diet, "detoxing," or emotionally hungover from the holidays—and you're over here trying to celebrate while it's dark at 5 p.m. Your gifts are wrapped in leftover Christmas paper, if you're lucky enough to get any. People will try to do the combo gift by leveling up the amount they would normally spend on your Christmas gift but still get a deal by not having to buy two. My first husband tried to pull this on our first married Christmas. He bought me the gorgeous Bulova watch I'd been eyeing that was certainly beyond our means.

A few weeks later, we celebrated my 20th birthday with a newborn. She was the best gift I ever received, even if she was a day late. And apparently, that was the only birthday gift I was getting that year.

So, come August, when his birthday rolled around, nada on a gift from me. When questioned, I simply replied, "Oh, remember that leather jacket I bought you for Christmas? It was more money than I was planning on spending. So, that was your birthday gift, too." *Pettylujah.* It never happened again.

To pile on the misery, it's January in Cleveland. Pool parties are out. On my 30th birthday, I spent 6 hours waiting for a tow during a blizzard because my car broke down on the highway. As if that weren't enough, the Somervilles' January birthday calendar is jam packed. We all know the people who celebrate their birthday month, yeah, that ain't flying in the Somerville family. We've got 10+ to celebrate. Overnight hotels stay for you. Upside, a lot of cake, you pick dinner, sit at the head of the table, and did I mention the cake? Meggie and I have never shared a birthday cake. No way. No how.

Downside: it's January. *Are you paying attention?*

Meggie and I both love sports, live music, sunshine, Disney, and a good French 75. She enjoys her alone time, is a deep thinker, expert problem solver. Although Meggie is nowhere near the diva I am, and she studied science instead of Shakespeare, in many ways, she is my mini-me—without all the traumas. Don't fret, I gave her plenty to talk to her therapist about – being my daughter isn't easy.

The one thing she did get from me is a tell it like it is attitude. Like me, she is an equal opportunity offender, although she's a bit less biting than I am – she leaves that to her patients.

She has no problem calling *me* on the carpet, especially now that we're two grown-ass adults.

Since I moved to Florida, we've maintained this connectivity through hilarious memes, live-text sports commentary during Browns games, and random questions or observations that let each other know we're thinking of one another. No context needed. Lines like "Um, I invented Post-Its" ala "Romey and Michelle's High School Reunion" or "Stupid Llama" ala "Dude Where's My Car". Bring a literal LOL.

It works for us. She's a millennial, and I'm a GenXer. *Ew, don't call.* Phone calls are for important things, things that do require context or because, you know what, it's been a while. We barely even FaceTime.

However, we try never go more than three months without seeing each other in-person and make sure we never leave each other without our next adventure planned. We found out quickly that "let me check my schedule and get back to you with some ideas" can result in almost eight months going by without seeing each other. It's usually a couple of quick trips for family things, a Browns game or concert, and our big trip. I may have moved to Florida because my life was happening right now, but that's right, my life is happening right now, and we only get one. Ohana.

I slotted NYC into that cadence. This was non-negotiable. Meggie had never been to NYC, and I hadn't since college and that was just a drive through on my way to a friend's beach house in Old Lyme, Connecticut. (Lucky Duck grew up on the beach!) I stalked the pre-sale dates, put it on my calendar, and procured third-row seats. My motto: life is too short to sit in shitty seats. I've done my time.

As I predicted, *Othello* on Broadway sold out so quickly that by the time it came around, it was truly the hottest ticket in town. Opening night was attended by former President and Dr. Biden. Later, the first female Vice President of the United States and First Gentleman. And so was that little girl from West Park who was told to sit down in the fifth grade for dreaming too big.

In my line of work, though, the subject of any trips coming up is standard in the small talk repertoire. And, even if you have nothing big planned, there is always something on the horizon. After all, we do live where people vacation: someone's always coming to visit. Disney can be a daytrip, and the beach can be visited frequently, if that's your thing. So, the topic of *Othello* on Broadway surfaced quite frequently in the year leading up to it. At first, it was just generally NYC and going to see a Broadway Play which often led to my line. *Fun fact, I'm a Shakespearean scholar...*

Now, I was saying it with conviction.

Although I had plenty of time, my therapist was monitoring my progress. Not letting me fall into my old habits: How am I possibly going to fit it all in? How much will it cost? A dash of panic attacks, a cup of procrastination, until I've run out of time and I'm frantically dusting the entire experience with that familiar "edge." Regret, remorse, and finally, justification—YOLO. I throw everything but the kitchen sink into that suitcase. At least it'll make a good story, if I only show the highlight reels. But now, I could add sprinkles and frosting— without the guilt that usually came with those empty calories I didn't need anyway.

After Chicago, eight months prior, I just wanted to feel that magic again. Was it lightning in a bottle, or was I really healing? *See it is me*—it fits both, doesn't it? I planned this one on purpose. Sure, I wanted it to look good—Insta-worthy, my outfits planned and on point, hashtags and captions ready to go, if I'm being honest. But I also wanted to actually be there this time. To live it. To stay in the present tense.

So, got out my planner, stickers and a note pad and made a list of all the things I wanted to do, and asked Meggie to do the same. We identified our non-negotiables, would-be great ifs, and our wishlist. Once compiled, I put my newly obtained certificate from the University of South Florida, *GenAI in Action: Impact and Possibilities,* to work. Add Chat GPT, my digital assistant, to my glam squad.

I used this initial prompt:

> "I am going to NYC with my adult daughter. We are going to see a Broadway Play on 4/19. Our travel dates are April 16-April 21st. In addition to the play, we would like to visit the 9/11 memorial, do a boat cruise to see the Statue of Liberty, and perhaps, another play. Would also like to go to Tiffany. It's Easter on Sunday, and I would like time to meet family for lunch. Play the role of a travel agent and suggest a hotel and itenerary. (sic). Keep in mind we've never been to NYC together, and our budget is modest, but we are bougie."

It gave me a framework to start with—one I refined as plans were confirmed or shifted to different days than Chatty-G had mapped out, like dinner at the Blue Box Café at Tiffany's. And when Meggie, who lives with a chef, added ideas—like a Michelin-starred restaurant where I ordered hot dogs topped with caviar—I folded those in too.

I was also very intentional about not overpacking the itinerary. I wanted room for spontaneity, enough sleep, and the freedom not to feel like we were constantly rushing to fit everything in.

It worked on paper—and surprisingly, I had a lot of fun doing it. I felt like I had everything covered. I packed with purpose, left my job at work, and my husband in good hands with his mother and sister visiting from Cleveland. This was a new twist for me. Setting boundaries. Not being on call, not checking in, and not planning my visitor's "perfect" vacation. I was going on my own.

Meggie arrived first in NYC, settled into the hotel, and tracked my moves via a play-by-play text chain. Once I finally arrived, we had a comedy of errors moment set to Benny Hill's Yakety *Sax* as we kept missing each other between the lobby and the room. Finally, reunited, as planned, we then headed to the rooftop speakeasy with a gorgeous view of the city that never sleeps, until last call.

Day 1: We put our timeline to the test. We met my cousin Marina (she's the baby in the Batman picture) and her boys for brunch (champagne and hashbrowns, of course) and walked around Central Park until our timed tickets to the 9/11 Memorial and Museum, followed by dinner reservations at Tiffany's Blue Box Café.

Our timeline failed us. While the average person might spend 2 hours at the 9/11 Memorial and Museum, we barely made it through half of it. So much to take in. So many stories to read. Not just from a historical perspective, but as a museum enthusiast and storyteller. We decided not to rush and would use one of our "downtime" slots to come back in a few days. But then, when the same thing happened at Tiffany's, not enough time for shopping. I realized at this rate, if we keep slotting things in other places, it would be *here I go-go-go again*.

I didn't let that happen.

Side note. This method of planning turned into a great teaching topic for how to use AI in our workplace. I even shared it with our executive team.

As I mentioned before, everyone can relate to planning a trip, so I used that example to walk them through the process— planning, refining, spotting AI hallucinations, and learning how to catch errors. Like anything, AI can be a very useful tool, but you must do the work for it to be effective. *Life doesn't come with a use-as-directed manual.*

I ended up only posting a couple of photos during our trip. My Betsey Johnson combat boots made for walking through Central Park, and the two of us, pre-gaming before *Othello*. A picture I framed when I got home because it also captured our incandescence perfectly.

And, of course, all those after-show pictures—from when we somehow ended up behind the barricades in the front row of the backstage waiting area—purely by happenstance. We waved to Denzel, got autographs, and actually talked to Jake Gyllenhaal. I told him, "You were great as Iago—and I would know, I studied Shakespeare in college."

And Meggie? "I've loved you since 'Donnie Darko.'" What Eddie Vedder is to me, Jake Gyllenhaal is to Meggie. Cherry on top! Guess lightning can strike twice.

But as memorable and ah-ma-zing as that was, this trip wasn't about the feed, it was about the feeling. About Meggie seeing me, about me seeing myself, not the filtered version, not the captioned one. The woman I'm still becoming, right here, right now. That quiet moment happened in the Met.

Visiting the Met is like visiting the Louvre. So much to take in that there was no way we were going to see it all, even if we had allotted more time. This could be a trip to NYC in and of itself for someone like me. I knew that going in, but as time started running short, that suffocating feeling started creeping in, my feet and hands began to tingle, *Breathe, Sharon, breathe.* My eye started to twitch. *Breathe, Sharon, breathe.* I felt nauseous. *Breathe. Sharon. breathe. Seriously, I'm in an art museum, why is this happening here?* My heart began to race, so I moved away from Meggie, trying to self-regulate. I didn't want to melt down in front of her.

However, she spotted me using my Apple watch to monitor my heart rate and the Calm app to guide my breathing. She knew what that meant.

"Are you okay Mom?" she asked.

"I'm fine. Honey. Just a little overwhelmed. Let's just sit here on this galley bench for a moment," I replied.

We quietly talked about the trajectory of Degas' work, and after a few moments, I felt well enough to move. Meggie however, sensing this wasn't enough, despite me telling her "I'm fine"(again) took my hand and said, "we have time for one more gallery if we're going to hit the Museum store (*a must!),* so let's go to the Cloisters gallery where they have all the church art that you love."

I chuckled, "Don't threaten me with a good time. I do love me some medieval church art."

The alters, the stained glass, the triptychs, the vestments, the symbolism, and the pomp and circumstance of it all. This will calm me right down.

Nope, I was still on the struggle bus. We sat down once again amongst the Unicorn tapestry collection, which includes the famous "The Unicorn in Captivity." I started to gently cry.

"What are you thinking about, Mom?" she said as she put her tiny hand in mine. *No, really, we both have tiny hands.*

"Ruthie and that beautiful homily Fr. Mark delivered about

how a death like hers was hard to understand. But life is like the back of a tapestry sometimes. A collection of completely unrelated threads that just don't make sense. But turn it over, and the threads come together to form a picture of great beauty. God sees the canvas even if or when we don't." Hmm, I thought.

"I'm fine now, kiddo. Let's go to the gift shop," I said as I stood up.

This time, I meant it.

In the afterglow of our trip, she's back in Ohio, I'm back in Florida, we were texting each other pictures we took, reminiscing about our favorite moments, when this came across my screen:

> *Seriously, the art museum was one of my favorites. Being able to tell you what I know since I didn't study art, and you being able to tell me the reason and the why, was really awesome. I wish we had more time there. When you have time in Cleveland, I would like to go back with you since we have such a history there. You are truly an inspiration, and I'm so happy to call you, my mom.*

And there it was. What I had been searching for my whole life. Peace, Safety, Love, Acceptance. It doesn't have to all make sense; I don't have to have all the answers. I can't always see it, and that's okay. My demons may continue to come around, but now I have the right tools to fight them off. I guess I really am a superhero.

Encore: I AM MINE

"I know I was born and I know that I'll die
The in between is mine"
- Pearl Jam, I Am Mine

I've been wanted to write this book for a very long time. In fact, I started it over ten years ago, but I just wasn't healthy enough to finish it (or anything else, apparently.) In combing through my endless notebooks, computer files, Post-Its, and even napkins of all those brilliant ideas I had, memories I wanted to capture, and ways to make it clever, I stumbled upon another book I started even before that one. It was titled *Thirty*.

It was intended to be a gift to my oldest nephew, also named Marty, on his thirtieth birthday (he's now in his 40s), and it was to contain 30 stories about his father.

I had them all mapped out but quickly scrapped this idea after writing a few chapters. It was far too close to his birthday to produce anything of quality. *Okay, I thought, no worries, he's got two younger brothers, I'll do it for them.* Nope. The youngest, AJ, is almost 40. Still unfinished. Another reminder of the stops and starts in my life. Proof of my failures.

Within that "book" is the following unedited story titled "Radar Love," which came from a blog I published in 2010, called Making Remarks.

The "About Me" says:

> I'm an ordinary girl with an extraordinary amount of interests and thoughts. Live, Love, Lake [another

blog I was writing] is about my DIY and craft projects, primarily inspired by my life on the shores of Lake Erie (Cleveland, OH) and my love of water. Making Remarks is about, well, my remarks on many things...primarily getting over the loss of my brother Marty.

I also first published "The Music Truck" story 'for my beautiful daughter Meghanne.' Retaining some level of naivety in life isn't necessarily a bad thing."

Here is Radar Love:

Long before Guitar Hero, kids got together in their bedrooms, blasted the music, and rocked out on their air instruments and sang at the top of their lungs. Marty and I were no exception.

Throughout the course of our lives, Marty and I shared many musical moments. Seeing Paul McCartney and Pink Floyd at the old Browns Stadium. Seeing The Who on their "farewell" tour in 1982 and David Bowie on his "Let's Dance" tour a year later. Listening to Genesis' *The Lamb Lies Down on Broadway* and Lynyrd Skynyrd's "Free Bird" and "Tuesday's Gone" around a Tidioute campfire. Even dancing on the bar at the Public House to Guns 'n Roses' "Paradise City" on my 25th birthday (and yes, there is a videotape!).

But there is one song that every time I hear it—it stops me dead in my tracks and transforms me into a child— Golden Earring's "Radar Love."

The image is so clear, like it was just yesterday. And it is, in fact, one of my earliest childhood memories and indeed one of the most vivid. Marty's bedroom circa 1973. So, I was no more than 4-5 years-old and Marty, a mere 10-11. He had the back bedroom at our home on Allien. There were three twin beds in the room at the time—most likely occupied also by Timmy and Ray. Posters all over the wall and clothes all over the floor.

But these posters were circa 1970s, and they were black light posters! And, that Christmas, Marty (or one of the boys) got not only a black light, but a strobe light as well! And the 45 record of Golden Earring's "Radar Love".

Marty and I would go up to his room. Turn out all the lights. Turn on the black light and the strobe light. Turn the volume all the way up on our portable turn-table. Drop the needle. And then we'd take our positions, start jumping on the bed, play our air guitars, and sing at the top of our lungs....

I've been drivin' all night, my hand's wet on the wheel....

We did this over and over and over again until finally "mom" would come upstairs and say... "turn that down and stop jumping on the beds! One of you are going to crack your head open!" (*she was right...eventually, one day while we were jumping on the beds, I did crack my head open! And I've got the scar to prove it! The one above my right eyebrow that drives my esthetician crazy every time I go in to get my brows done.*)

Needless to say. Every time I hear "Radar Love," I turn it up as loud as possible, and sometimes, I even jump on the bed.

Even in writing this book, I've rewrote this passage a few times (hello, perfectionist right here), put it in other chapters, pulled it out entirely, but ultimately decided to save it for the encore. Exactly the way I wrote it the first time, because it wasn't the story I needed to rewrite; it was all the triggers that came with it. The unhealed pain, the unresolved trauma, the lingering self-doubt, the feeling that I was never enough.

Now look at me, I made it to the finish line. Woo-Hoo! Content with this version of me and every other version I am and will become.

While I may have at one time thought like Jo Marsh, "I should have been a great many things." Today, I recognize I already am and that there is absolutely nothing wrong with being an ordinary girl with an extraordinary amount of interests and thoughts, who organizes her life with stickers and stickies, surrounds herself with pretty things, and stomps around life in fabulous footwear.

I am Batman. I am a Shakespearean scholar. I am a Disney Adult. I am a non-profit visionary, and ultimately, I'm just a girl who loves Pearl Jam. I am mine.

Future Days

The Uber Black dropped us in front of the sleek white jet waiting on the tarmac. Marc, Butters, and I climbed the air stairs while the co-pilot grabbed our bags. As Marc and Butters get settled, I visit the cockpit, carrying a Tiffany-blue gift bag with its white rope handles brushing softly against my wrist.

"Hey Kiddo, thanks for picking us up," I say as I kiss the pilot on the head and take the co-pilot's spot.

"Anything for you Mimi," says my grandson, Caden. "We had a deal."

I pull a small teddy bear out of the bag, "Look what I picked up for baby Rose. Isn't it precious?"

"Definitely a Mimi gift!" he says with a smile.

The flight attendant pops in and asks me to take my seat. "Your usual Mrs. Boyes?" she asks as she places the shopping bag the in the overhead bin.

"You know it! Champagne and HashBrowns!"

Cheers

Coda:
When the House Lights Go Up

Lessons from the Road

1. Action Alleviates Anxiety

2. Education Is Empowerment

3. Strive for *Pearlfection*, Not Perfection

4. Comparison Is the Thief of Joy

5. Happiness and Joy Are Two Very Different Things

6. Don't React—Respond

7. Create Space, Not Just Time, for What Matters Most

8. Pain Is Not a Competition

9. Not Everything That Sparkles Is Superficial

10. Survival Was the Beginning—Not the Goal

The Soundtrack

1. Invincible — Eddie Vedder
2. Given to Fly — Pearl Jam
3. The Real Me — The Who
4. Thumbing My Way — Pearl Jam
5. Sunshower — Chris Cornell
6. Tiny Dancer — Elton John
7. And So It Goes — Billy Joel
8. Don't Give Up — Peter Gabriel (feat. Kate Bush)
9. Walk — Foo Fighters
10. Indifference — Pearl Jam

Acknowledgements

THIS BOOK WAS written in pieces—on long drives, in quiet kitchens, and in the spaces between who I was and who I was becoming. It's held together by people, music, and moments that refused to let me disappear. Thank you.

To my readers: Reading changed my life. If this book connects with just one person, it's done its job.

To the women who didn't know they were saving me: Meg Benson, Erin Blankenship, Val Brinkley, Margarete Cassalina, Cindy Duber, Casey Evert, Sharon Fekete, Sara Lorz, Sarah Melamed, Lisa Mullin, Lindsay Petty, Kelly Pyper, Jessica Rivelli, Christine Sabo, Carolyn Sekerak. The entire Pearl Jam 10c Women Members, especially Robyn Metz.

To the Somerville Family: This list is so long, I'm going to quit while I'm ahead. If you weren't mentioned in this book, please don't feel left out. I'm just getting started. I love each one of you. I hit the family lottery being born a Somerville.

I do, however, want to share this text I sent to Ray:

> I certainly wouldn't have survived or be the woman I am without you. From giving me a safe space always, to buying my college textbooks and wedding dress, to ruining the Music Truck ruse with my daughter (if you don't remember that—the story is in the book), to shouldering responsibilities that should have been mine when my mental health just couldn't take it anymore.

To my West Park Family: Heather, Margaret, Lisa, Barb, and the Williams, Nagle, and O'Donnell clans. The Ferchill family. All my sisters from SJA (Kelly, Chrissie, Jen, Carol, Annie, Stephanie...I'm going to stop there so I don't leave anyone out!) and all our friends at the all-boys schools (St. Eds and St. Ignatius). You know who you are!

To my John Carroll University grad school crew, whose "rowdiness" while listening to Frank Sinatra and crafting puppets resulted in a visit from the police after a noise complaint—you are my people. Tina, Steve, Kathleen, Todd, Amy, Juliet, Stephanie, and Senn. Dawn and Marcie, I love you too.

To Ruthie. I saw a glimpse of your pain, and that was enough. I will still never understand your choice, but it was yours. I respect and honor that every single day of my life.

To my children, Meggie, Keith, Jarod, and Alex (Jodi). You are my everything.

My grandchildren, Caden, Kathleen, and baby J.

To Marty's children, spouses, and children: Marty, Kelly, Mara, Evie, Brian, Rachel, a player to be named later, AJ, April, Joseph, and my goddaughter, Rosie. Having you in my life gives me a piece of your father back every day. He is so proud of all of you.

To the exes who believed in creating a family. Period. Abandoning words like blended or step and putting the children first. Thank you, Jean Ann, Gordon (Kathy), and Colleen. It wasn't always easy, it wasn't always perfect, but we did good.

To my professional anchors who believed in me and opened doors, knowing full well about my spiciness: Steve Csenge, Stacey Efaw, Steve Millard, Scott Simon, and Michelle Turman. And the late Vic Gelb, Allan Krulak, and Valerie McCormack.

To all of my favorite bands and literary authors—concerts, records, books, dog-eared paperbacks, deep cuts, and passages too numerous to name—you saved me. You gave me home when I felt unmoored, and hope when I wasn't sure where to find it. I have done everything in my power to quote and credit lyrics, texts, and creators properly. Any artwork, stickers, or visual elements appearing in this book or on its cover are from my personal collection or are original to the author.

To my editors, early readers, designers, therapists and teachers (named or unnamed), and those who helped shape the work itself: Rachel Kray, Grace-Anne Alfiero, Elizabeth Nici, my psychiatrist Dr. B, my therapist Jami, the late Dr. Christopher Roark for introducing me to Shakespeare, and Dr. MaryClaire Moroney for teaching me how to analyze it and find my academic voice.

And finally, to my favorite and personal rock star, my husband Marc.

Long Live Rock.

Some Of Us Show Up Already Wearing the Costume.